IMMIGRATION

**GREAT
SPEECHES
IN
HISTORY**

Michelle E. Houle,
Book Editor

Daniel Leone, *President*

Bonnie Szumski, *Publisher*

Scott Barbour, *Managing Editor*

David M. Haugen, *Series Editor*

GREENHAVEN
PRESS®

THOMSON

━━━━★━━━━™

GALE

San Diego • Detroit • New York • San Francisco • Cleveland
New Haven, Conn. • Waterville, Maine • London • Munich

Cover credit: © Bettmann/CORBIS
Library of Congress, 44, 54, 67

LIBRARY OF CONGRESS CATALOGING-IN-PUBLICATION DATA
Immigration / Michelle E. Houle, book editor.
p. cm. — (Greenhaven Press's great speeches in history)
Includes bibliographical references and index.
ISBN 0-7377-1874-9 (lib. : alk. paper) — ISBN 0-7377-1875-7 (pbk. : alk. paper)
1. United States—Emigration and immigration. 2. History—20th century.
3. United States—Government policy. 4. Speeches, addresses, etc. I. Houle,
Michelle E. II. Great speeches in history series.
E185.61. H5913 2004
323.2-73.—dc21   2003

Printed in the United States of America

Contents

are but a few examples of immigrants whose presence has greatly enriched the United States.

Chapter 2: Voices Opposed to Increased or Unregulated Immigration

Jewish people the process would be tantamount to a death sentence. For those who wish to end Jewish immigration into the United States, the answer is to create a home country for Jewish people.

Chapter 4: The Impact of Immigration

Only through tolerance can the nation progress and prosper.

Foreword

I have a dream that one day this nation will rise up and live out the true meaning of its creed: "We hold these truths to be self-evident: that all men are created equal."

I have a dream that one day on the red hills of Georgia the sons of former slaves and the sons of former slave owners will be able to sit down together at the table of brotherhood.

I have a dream that one day even the state of Mississippi, a state sweltering with the heat of injustice, sweltering with the heat of oppression, will be transformed into an oasis of freedom and justice.

I have a dream that my four little children will one day live in a nation where they will not be judged by the color of their skin but by the content of their character.

Perhaps no speech in American history resonates as deeply as Martin Luther King Jr.'s "I Have a Dream," delivered in 1963 before a rapt audience of 250,000 on the steps of the Lincoln Memorial in Washington, D.C. Decades later, the speech still enthralls those who read or hear it, and stands as a philosophical guidepost for contemporary discourse on racism.

What distinguishes "I Have a Dream" from the hundreds of other speeches given during the civil rights era are King's eloquence, lyricism, and use of vivid metaphors to convey abstract ideas. Moreover, "I Have a Dream" serves not only as a record of history—a testimony to the racism that permeated American society during the 1960s—but it is also a historical event in its own right. King's speech, aired live on national television, marked the first time that the grave injustice of racism was fully articulated to a mass audience in a way that was both logical and evocative. Julian Bond, a fellow participant in the civil rights movement and student of King's, states that

> King's dramatic 1963 "I Have a Dream" speech before the Lincoln Memorial cemented his place as first among equals in civil rights leadership; from this first televised mass meeting, an American audience saw and heard the unedited oratory of America's finest preacher, and for the first time, a mass white audience heard the undeniable justice of black demands.

Moreover, by helping people to understand the justice of the civil rights movement's demands, King's speech helped to transform the nation. In 1964, a year after the speech was delivered, President Lyndon B. Johnson signed the Civil Rights Act, which outlawed segregation in public facilities and discrimination in employment. In 1965, Congress passed the Voting Rights Act, which forbids restrictions, such as literacy tests, that were commonly used in the South to prevent blacks from voting. King's impact on the country's laws illustrates the power of speech to bring about real change.

Greenhaven Press's Great Speeches in History series offers students an opportunity to read and study some of the greatest speeches ever delivered before an audience. Each volume traces a specific historical era, event, or theme through speeches— both famous and lesser known. An introductory essay sets the stage by presenting background and context. Then a collection of speeches follows, grouped in chapters based on chronology or theme. Each selection is preceded by a brief introduction that offers historical context, biographical information about the speaker, and analysis of the speech. A comprehensive index and an annotated table of contents help readers quickly locate material of interest, and a bibliography serves as a launching point for further research. Finally, an appendix of author biographies provides detailed background on each speaker's life and work. Taken together, the volumes in the Greenhaven Great Speeches in History series offer students vibrant illustrations of history and demonstrate the potency of the spoken word. By reading speeches in their historical context, students will be transported back in time and gain a deeper understanding of the issues that confronted people of the past.

Introduction: Speaking Out on Immigration

When Jose Gutierrez was eight years old, he and another homeless orphan decided to escape the poverty of Guatemala City and cross the border into the United States. The boys hopped a northbound train and got themselves smuggled into California, where they eventually made their way to Los Angeles. There they parted company. Jose was placed with a Los Angeles foster family who eventually adopted him, and to whom he confided his hope to save enough money to retrieve his sister from Guatemala City. He also expressed a desire to repay the country that had provided him with a home and family. Jose enlisted in the U.S. Marine Corps and, unfortunately, made history as one of the first casualties in the war on Iraq. Jose and a select group of slain immigrant marines were awarded posthumous citizenship when their bodies were returned to the United States.

After reporting this story, the anchorman for a national news broadcast, Tom Brokaw, followed his report with these words: "A story to remember the next time you're tempted to rail against the immigrants coming into this country."[1] What motivated him to speak out on the issue is a sentiment that has been felt by people in the United States for centuries—a strong sense of the importance of weighing in on an issue that enjoys no consensus in public opinion.

Public sentiment about immigration has gone through many changes in the nation's history. Questions about citizenship, ethnicity, and economics have played a part in the historical discourse on immigration, and heated debates on these issues continue today. In the study of U.S. immigration history, the sheer volume of source material available is overwhelming. Statistics from national censuses, first-person immigrant narratives, vessel rosters, materials from advocacy groups, and many more research tools can be found easily in libraries and on the Internet. This anthology compiles speeches on immigration. Such public addresses are helpful because they provide unique records of the specific issues relating to immigration that trouble each generation of Americans. Speeches also convey the sense of moral propriety generally held by the different sides of the polemic issues that surround immigration policy.

The platforms for speaking out on immigration have changed throughout U.S. history, and whether in a church or a courtroom, the physical location of a speech is part of the argument being made. The audience, type of forum, political climate, and current events all influence speeches and the debates on immigration.

What Immigration Is

In its simplest definition, immigration is the process of leaving one's home country to resettle in a new one. A person is an immigrant *to* a country, and an emigrant or émigré *from* a country. People who have escaped from situations of war, fear of persecution, or other recognized disasters often apply for immigration to the United States as refugees. The channels through which foreign nationals enter the country are either legal or illegal. Legal means of entry include approved requests for visas and birth on U.S. soil. Illegal means include failure to leave upon expiration of legal visas and smuggling. These are definitions undisputed by historians. However, there is no clear consensus regarding the official start date of American immigration. Does one begin with Kennewick man? Spanish colonists? the Pilgrims? This is the first controversy one finds when delving into American immigration history.

Americans Pre-1815

Indigenous peoples already populated American territory when European explorers began their voyages of conquest.

To many natives, the European emigration was unsolicited and unwelcome. In 1565 Spaniards established Saint Augustine, Florida, as the first known settlement in North America. Spanish immigrants arrived in parts of the Southwest in 1598, and in 1607 English settlers colonized Jamestown, Virginia. In a 1629 message designed for an audience unfamiliar with indigenous people, the Reverend Francis Higginson described the inhabitants of New England as follows: "For their governors they have kings. . . . The men for the most part live idly, they do nothing but hunt and fish. Their wives set their corn and do all their other work. They have little household stuff, as a kettle, and some other vessels like trays, spoons, dishes and baskets. . . . Their houses are very little and homely."[2] Higginson's description gives an idea of how different the native people were to the European colonizers. The distinctions made it easy for the Europeans to think of the natives as savages, as the "other."

The introduction and subsequent waves of British colonists proved catastrophic for native peoples, many of whom died from illnesses introduced by the Europeans. As a result, disease and conquest altered and destroyed most Native American societies. And the Europeans became the dominant stock in the new land.

Since its inception as a nation, America has peopled itself with immigrants. The racial and ethnic composition of each wave of immigrants is and has been historically diverse. The first African American immigrants were forcibly relocated to Jamestown, Virginia, in 1619, and this population grew to approximately five hundred thousand by the beginning of the Revolutionary War. By the mid–eighteenth century, the colonies established along the eastern seaboard were owned by England, but even there the English did not dominate America's ethnic composition. According to historian Jon Gjerde, "The bulk of immigrants in the eighteenth century did not come from England . . . [and] people of English ancestry composed less than one-half of the population in 1790."[3] The diversity of people in the colonies still were under English rule, even if they spoke Dutch or German. The colonists, therefore, needed to find ways to communicate and live together. But for many immigrants, the primary needs were still food and shelter.

In this era the pulpit served as the primary platform for debate on immigration. In 1797, for example, Unitarian minister Joseph Priestley, whose family had fled religious persecution in England, delivered a sermon to appeal for the creation of a public institution to serve the needs of recent immigrants. His Philadelphia church was widely attended, and he hoped that his printed and circulated argument in support of social accommodation and financial assistance for immigrants would find a sympathetic audience in his congregation and beyond.

The First Great Wave, 1815–1924

From 1815 until the restrictions of 1924, millions of immigrants embarked on the journey to America to settle in a land that seemed to offer freedom and opportunity. Many died en route, and of those who arrived, many encountered the hardships faced by previous immigrants. They had no place to go or were struggling to find basic necessities. In a report argued before the New York city council in 1847, the commissioner of a poorhouse described the miserable first experiences common to multitudes of immigrants:

> Large numbers of these unfortunate emigrants, as soon as they quit the decks of their vessels, having no home to which to direct their movements, wander through the streets in a state of utter desolation, until some benevolent hand, appalled by the misery and wretchedness before him, guides their prostrated frames and tottering gait to the Park almshouse board; and here is exhibited so sickening a picture of human destitution and suffering. . . . The deplorable infirmity of their desolate unhappiness must be *seen and felt*, to be appreciated; and then, to often find amid the motley groups some with the last gasp of expiration issuing from their cold and blanched lips, forms a scene of dismay and distress too agonizing to look upon with any other than feelings of horror and overwhelming sympathy. . . . "Leaving their homes," they say, "with the brightest of prospects," alluring representations presented to them of the blessed state of American life, a few scanty coins in their pockets, though feeling in the enjoyment of

rugged health and surrounded by their young and innocent offspring, little did they imagine the trials to which they would be exposed, but at length they discover to their sorrow, and very natural discontent, that the foul steerage of some ocean-tossed ship is to form the receptacle of their persons, crowded too with hordes of human beings, with scarcely enough space to contain the half of them . . . ; and thus huddled together *en masse*, they become the emigrant passengers destined to this country. Numbers of them . . . fall victim to the destroying contagion, and the ocean wave becomes their silent tomb; and when at length our shores are reached, many of them had far better have been cast into the "deep sea," than linger in the pangs of hunger, sickness, and pain, to draw their last agonizing breath in the streets of New York.[4]

The passengers on these immigrant vessels headed for the United States fled famine, wars, and desperate poverty in hopes of a new life in the promise of America.

Reactions to New Americans

Many of the people described in the almshouse commissioner's report were emigrants from Great Britain, western Europe, and Ireland. The Irish immigrants started arriving en masse in the 1840s after a brutal potato famine devastated the nation. Chinese immigrants first arrived in California around 1848, and at the same time Germans emigrated to escape political conflict. According to the U.S. Department of State, roughly 34 million people immigrated to the United States in the hundred years between 1820 and 1920, and approximately three-fourths of them stayed. This massive influx of immigrants filled factory jobs and populated the cities. However, many people grew to resent these new laborers, who were often desperate enough to work for the lowest wages. Resident factory workers viewed immigrants as a threat to their livelihoods. Fears that ethnic minorities would somehow compromise American culture also factored in to a sense of panic concerning the newcomers. Economic issues combined with culture clashes and xenophobia swelled "nativist" or anti-immigrant sentiment in the mid– and late nineteenth century.

In the 1850s the popularity of the Know-Nothing movement, an anti-immigrant secret society and political party, reached its peak. Members of this organization got their name by refusing to answer questions about their affiliation with the party, instead answering, "I know nothing." Anti-immigration advocates argued that immigration threatened the nation's political structure because immigrants were ill informed on the issues and, in some cases, not mentally competent to vote. It was also feared that Catholic immigrants would place higher loyalty to the pope than to the U.S. government. In addition, individual ethnic groups were accused of political radicalism and specific character flaws such as avarice and sloth.

The Chinese Exclusion Act of 1882 was another product of anti-immigrant nativism. This law prohibited the immigration of Chinese laborers (who worked cheaply), and some politicians bluntly admitted the perceived "evil" of Chinese immigration. One historian writes that the passage of this act "became the hinge on which the 'golden door' of immigration began to swing closed."[5] Nine years later, Congress passed the Immigration Act of 1891, the first of its kind, which created a Bureau of Immigration controlled by the Department of the Treasury and mandated the deportation of illegal aliens.

In 1896 Henry Cabot Lodge introduced a bill that cut immigration levels in order to maintain racial balances, and proposed admittance based on literacy tests and an immigrant tax. Although this bill did not succeed, literacy tests became a popular topic of debate and twenty-one years later, the literacy test passed as a provision of the 1917 Immigration Act. Not all advocates of reduced immigration were racists, but unabashedly racist opponents to immigration cited Anglo-Saxon superiority as the reason for eliminating or restricting immigration. Others opposed what they saw as the polluting of American culture by immigrant customs and traditions.

Economic Development and Immigration

Opponents of immigrant restrictions, however, did not always have altruistic motives. Some saw an economic opportunity in the recruitment of new immigrants as cheap labor. Debate over the net economic costs and benefits of immigration took place in a variety of forums. In an 1849 address before the Agricultural Society of Lewis County, New York, U.S. representative Charles Clarke lauded the promise of inexpensive labor. He argued,

> If despite the thousand labour-saving machines which your ingenuity has invented, labour bears too high a price—call on the foreigner to come to your aid, to share your toils, to divide your labour, and enjoy your free and equal laws. Receive him kindly—remember that his forefathers and yours were brethren, that your forefathers once were foreigners, and that time was, when the only "native American" was a wild Indian. Let ignorance, prejudice, and exclusiveness carp and criticize and find fault as they may, the immigrants coming from the teeming millions of Europe, are immeasurably the most valuable importations we make.[6]

While business leaders and proponents of free enterprise sensed opportunity, black southern workers, including freed slaves, sensed unfair competition. In the 1850s and 1860s, Germans, Scandinavians, and Chinese emigrated in large numbers, most seeking jobs in the factories of the North. But, increasingly, new immigrant labor pools migrated toward the southern states, to the delight of growers and farm owners. The requirement that citizens must be "free" and "white" established by the Naturalization Act of 1790 denied full citizenship rights to African Americans until 1870. The disenfranchised black population of the South, however, continued to grow in these years (despite anti-slave-smuggling legislation, historians have noted that slave traders illegally transported as many as fifty thousand slaves into the United States between 1808 and 1865). In opposition to the importation of foreign nationals as workers, the freed blacks of the South feared that the immigrant population would displace them from their homes and jobs. In this often cited quotation from his speech delivered at the Atlanta Exposition of 1895, African American advocate Booker T. Washington argues, "To those of the white race who look to the incoming of those of foreign birth and strange tongue and habits for the prosperity of the South, were I permitted I would repeat what I say to my own race, 'Cast down your bucket where you are.'"[7] The unique impact of immigration on African Americans continued to be a hotly disputed issue and remains one today. Some prominent scholars conclude that the hiring of immigrants perpetuates racist hiring practices and lowers wages for black workers; others argue that the inference that black workers only compete for the low-wage jobs usually held by immigrants is insulting.

The public face of U.S. immigration took a giant leap forward when in 1886 President Grover Cleveland dedicated the Statue of Liberty, an iconic symbol of American ideology. For many of the millions who immigrated to the United States, this statue was their first glimpse of America, and the famous poem carved on the pedestal by Jewish American Emma Lazarus emblemized the promise of American economic, political, and religious freedom. In 1892 the Immigration and Naturalization Service opened Ellis Island in New York as a way station for screening the multitudes of new arrivals. More than 10 million immigrants arrived on U.S. soil between 1905 and 1914.

Quotas and Restrictions, 1924–1965

The public anxiety triggered by this influx of people influenced lawmakers in the direction of anti-immigration legislation. The backlash against immigrants enjoyed a swell of popularity that culminated with the Johnson-Reed Act, also known as the Immigration Act of 1924. Using 1910 census figures to determine "appropriate" percentages of immigrants from each foreign land, this landmark legislation established strict quotas on those who could legally become citizens. In this manner, only 3 percent of "desirable" nationality head counts would be accepted. The thrust of this law, according to historian Roger Daniels, "was undisguised ethnic discrimination directed largely against people from southern and eastern Europe . . . [and] Asians were not allowed to immigrate, except for Filipinos, who were American nationals."[8] This mathematical formulation to determine desirable ethnic categories for immigration remained law until its repeal by Lyndon Johnson in 1965. America had shifted from a country that had aggressively encouraged immigration in its formative years to a population convinced that enough was enough.

Aspects of the Immigration Debate Midcentury

Despite the national restrictions, some organizations in America sought to help immigrants who were allowed into the country. Benevolent societies and mutual aid associations emerged in the larger cities, especially in ethnic cities and neighborhoods, by the beginning of the twentieth century. The meeting halls of these clubs became popular forums for discussions on issues facing immigrants, as well as good places to address problems particular to immigrant communities. Racism and scapegoating of immigrants as menaces and detriments to society were significant dilemmas faced by ethnic minorities. In this hostile climate to immigrants, social activists such as Jane Addams worked as important intermediaries between the often-misunderstood ethnic poor and their working-class neighbors. To audiences of politicians, social workers, academics, and residents of her settlement houses, Addams championed the message that immigrants are hardworking people with as much value for human life as native-born citizens.

Anti-immigrant bias, however, remained pervasive, and even courtrooms were not immune. One of the most famous speeches ever delivered by an immigrant can be found in the transcripts of the notorious trial of Sacco and Vanzetti. In a Dedham, Massachusetts, courtroom in 1921, Italian immigrants and anarchists Nicola Sacco and Bartolomeo Vanzetti asserted their innocence in a murder and robbery case and declared that they were denied a fair trial due to prejudice against their immigrant lineage and political beliefs. Vanzetti delivered a speech after his conviction that is profoundly eloquent in its tortured English:

> This is what I say: I would not wish to a dog or a snake, to the most low and misfortunate creature of the earth—I would not wish to any of them what I have had to suffer for things that I am not guilty of. But my conviction is that I have suffered for things that I am guilty of. I am suffering

because I am a radical, and indeed I am a radical; I have suffered because I was an Italian, and indeed I am an Italian.[9]

It is commonly believed that the two men were scapegoated,
and that their unpopular political affiliation helped jurors see
them as foreign troublemakers. For their alleged crime, Sacco
and Vanzetti were executed in 1927. Proponents of liberalizing
immigration measures seized on the monumental travesty of
this case, which received worldwide attention for its injustice.

Crises of Conscience: Jews, Asians, and Mexicans in America

Marked growth in the numbers of private organizations and
women's clubs increased the arenas available for people who
wished to speak out on immigration, and many of these social clubs aspired to educate their members. In the late 1930s
a massive population of Jews and non-Jews fled the Third
Reich in Nazi Germany, and as a result of restrictionist legislation and anti-Semitic propaganda, large numbers of these
refugees (including Jewish children) were denied admittance
to the United States. In 1939 journalist Dorothy Thompson
felt compelled to address this issue, and chose the American
Federation of Women's Clubs as her forum. Thompson urged
women to pay careful attention to the sources of information
and statistics they receive about immigrants. "People are being told that this country is being flooded with refugees," she
asserted. "Actually, this is pure and simple malicious propaganda and not in the least in harmony with the facts. The
facts are that the American immigration quotas have not
been extended at all, while the conditions under which one
can get a quota number have been made more rigorous. Only
42,685 persons entered the United States last year from all
the countries of the world . . . and in the six years from 1932
to 1938, 4,487 more aliens left this country than were admitted under the immigration laws."[10]

Another troubling issue of the time directly affected
people of Asian heritage who lived in the United States. Public misconceptions about the loyalty of Asian Americans during World War II led to fear and discrimination against citizens and others of Asian descent. In 1942 the internment of

Japanese in America living on the West Coast began in the wake of the surprise attack on Pearl Harbor. On February 16, President Roosevelt signed Executive Order 9066, which authorized the rounding up of thousands of Japanese Americans and their forced relocation into resettlement camps. Many Japanese American families remained in these camps until the end of the war. This action was later legitimized by Congress in Title II of the International Security Act of 1950. When Congress finally debated a reparation package for the survivors of this tragedy in 1988, Senator Daniel Inouye noted how racism factored in to a measure purportedly created in the interest of national security:

> While it is true that all people of this Nation suffer during wartime, the Japanese-American internment experience is unprecedented in the history of American civil rights deprivation. I think we should recall, even if painful, that Americans of Japanese ancestry were determined by our Government to be security risks without any formal allegations or charges of disloyalty or espionage. They were arbitrarily branded disloyal solely on the grounds of racial ancestry.
>
> No similar mass internment was deemed necessary for Americans of German or Italian ancestries, and I think we should recall and remind ourselves that in World War II, the Japanese were not our only enemies.
>
> These Japanese Americans who were interned could not confront their accusers or bring their case before a court. These are basic rights of all Americans. They were incarcerated, forced to live in public communities with no privacy, and stripped of their freedom to move about as others could.[11]

Yet another crisis of this era targeted Mexican Americans and individuals of Mexican descent. In order to supplement the labor shortage created by World War II deployments, the United States imported workers from Mexico through an agreement called the bracero program. The presence of braceros, the name given to the imported laborers, aggravated opponents of Mexican immigration, and in the summer of 1954 the Immigration and Naturalization Service (INS) launched a campaign to deport undocumented Mexican workers called "Operation Wetback." Officials of the INS combed Mexican neighborhoods and made identification checks on people who "looked Mexican," despite protests by social leaders such as Cesar Chavez. Although the campaign was devised to alleviate illegal immigration along the Mexican American border, in practice the INS routinely deported legal citizens. In the following three years, more than 2 million Mexicans and Mexican Americans were forcibly deported.

Another important piece of legislation had preceded Operation Wetback, the McCarran-Walter Act of 1952 (commonly referred to as the Immigration and Nationality Act). This act proposed to reaffirm the national origins quotas established in 1924. The measure also aimed to create new political tests for immigrants, expand the authority of the Border Patrol, and amend the guidelines concerning the reunification of families. In a speech taken from the congressional debate of the act, Senator Hubert Humphrey, who opposed the measure, credited the varied composition of Americans and the distinctly American mélange of cultural patterns and diversity with strengthening the foundations of society. He stated:

> I would remind Americans who proudly claim 100 percent Americanism that a study of the great cultural patterns of this nation will reveal what all of us have known to be true, namely, that we are a composite of the peoples of the world. Our country in a sense is a melting pot but not to the point where we have melted out our differences or cultural diversity. We have preserved the uniqueness and the flavor of different nationality groups and cultural patterns and social customs which have given America the unique beauty and strength which no other nation on earth possesses.[12]

Despite a veto by President Harry S. Truman, the act enjoyed tremendous support from Congress, and eventually passed. Immigration tides ebbed, and in 1954 Ellis Island was closed due to lack of use.

Immigration Policy After 1965

With the presidency of John F. Kennedy came a shift in thought about the role of immigrants and immigration in

American society. Kennedy, an Irish American, embraced his ancestry. He proposed an end to the national origins quota system on the grounds that immigrants are a source of strength for industry, the economy, and American culture. Kennedy did not live to see changes made, but Lyndon Johnson signed the Immigration and Nationality Act amendments in 1965, and a new and more pluralistic era in immigration history began.

In the 1960s more than nine hundred thousand refugees fled war-torn Indochina, and large numbers of Cubans began fleeing the regime of Cuban dictator Fidel Castro. The Refugee Act of 1980 established the first official system for admitting refugees, amended the official definition of who could be considered a refugee, and outlined procedures to assist displaced persons with domestic resettlement. The disparate nature of U.S. admission policies toward refugees is well illustrated by the examples of Cuba and Haiti. While close to 1 million Cuban refugees have been granted unique status and assisted financially, a substantially smaller number of Haitian refugees have been granted admission.

Scholars and historians do not often agree on the impact of these new immigrants; restrictionists cite detrimental effects to the economy, while pluralists contradict these figures with statistics of their own. According to researcher Steven A. Camarota and the Center for Immigration Studies, "Immigration in the 1970s lowered the wages of high school dropouts by between 10 and 16 percent annually ($2,250 to $3,800) and, in the 1980s, immigration primarily affected employment, with between 128,000 and 195,000 natives in California either unemployed or withdrawn from the labor force because of immigration."[13] Others argue that immigrants contribute financially by creating jobs through business ventures as well as through taxpaying and the purchase of consumer goods. In response to the perceived renewed economic and cultural threat posed by immigration, in the 1980s another phase of hand-wringing over "the immigrant problem" began.

In 1986 Congress passed the Immigration Reform and Control Act, which criminalized the hiring of illegal immigrants and provided a onetime amnesty for immigrants who had lived in the United States continuously for the past four years. Two years later, three states—Arizona, Colorado, and Florida—passed initiatives that declared English as the official state language. In 1994 controversial California Proposition 187 proposed to bar undocumented immigrants from public education and social services and deny them medical attention. This and other English-only initiatives gathered nationwide attention and inspired vocal debates on the effectiveness of certain measures conceived to help curb illegal immigration. Pat Buchanan ran for president in 1992 on a campaign platform centered on the issue of immigration—specifically, a crackdown on illegal immigration and a massive reduction of the total amount of entrance visas granted to prospective immigrants per year. Without these measures, Buchanan predicted the fracturing of America into ethnic enclaves.

Modern Forums on Immigration

Immigration is an intrinsic part of American history and an identifiable characteristic of the nation. Important decisions on U.S. policy have traced their genesis historically to churches, street corners, clubs, exposition halls, oratorical contests, and campaign trails. In other words, public gatherings have been the places where traditionally much of the debate has taken place on the issues related to immigration. For example, in an 1896 college oratorical contest, Native American Zitkala-Sä contemplated the consequences to Native Americans of the continental conquest by European explorers, and lamented the subsequent invasion of immigrants. Debating teams of 1914 chose to argue the efficacy and necessity of literacy tests. Radio and television editorials emerged midcentury as new mediums with which to voice opinions. In the 1960s and '70s ethnic pride movements took their messages of cultural empowerment to the streets. And universities and college campuses have been and continue to be fertile grounds for debates, places where speakers find built-in audiences for their addresses.

In 1994, political activist Raul Yzaguirre seized the opportunity of a commencement address to speak against stereotypes of immigrants. He contended,

America is of two minds when it comes to immigrants. On the one hand, we are proud of our immigrant heritage, symbolized by that great American icon known as the Statue of Liberty. Yet public opinion, going back as far as the early 1800s, has been decidedly against each new wave of immigrants. . . . We also know that economic security fuels our worst fears and brings out our meanest instincts. During every single recession, and especially during the great depression, the United States implemented policies that should bring shame to all of us. While precise figures are hard to come by, we can confidently estimate that well over one million legal immigrants and American citizens have been illegally and unjustly deported during economic downturns.[14]

Yzaguirre referenced biases held against Hispanics and Latinos in his speech and spoke in opposition to the waves of immigrant bashing that have periodically ebbed and flowed throughout U.S. history.

Twenty-First-Century Wars and Immigration

Since the events of September 11, 2001, the issue of immigration has almost become synonymous with security concerns. Experts on immigration such as immigration lawyers and reform lobbyists disagree wildly on how best to balance public safety and constitutional rights. Almost immediately after the tragedy occurred, New York mayor Rudy Giuliani spoke to the country about the dangers of anti-Arab sentiment and warned against misguided retribution toward Arabs and Arab Americans. Even though the perpetrators of the attack were not technically immigrants, policy watchers noted that the "INS came under intense scrutiny" and "critics of the agency took center stage."[15] It did not help matters when the agency approved the visa application for one of the hijackers after the fact. The war on terrorism expedited the demise (on paper at least) of an agency overwrought with complaints about mismanagement for decades. The name *INS* was officially abandoned in 2003 and a new division of the Department of Homeland Security was created to handle the duties of the old agency.

The most popular platform for both critics and proponents of U.S. immigration policy is the Internet. Public speakers are able to broaden their audiences by using the Internet to post the texts of their speeches, and in general the World Wide Web has revolutionized the way people inform themselves on changes in immigration policy and international matters relating to immigration.

Since the beginning of the war on Iraq in 2003, U.S. immigration policy is changing more rapidly than ever. Newly created Homeland Security detention centers and immigration checkpoints for foreign-born travelers (and those who resemble them) have grown in number. These new rules for detaining suspected violators of immigration policy encroach on civil liberties, according to some experts, and do not do enough, according to others. We have yet to comprehend the ramifications of detaining Arabs and Arab American citizens at the Guantánamo Bay military detention center without a trial, and only history will prove if this has been a prudent exercise in national security or a historical blight reminiscent of the 1940s internment camps. In another twist currently inspiring debate, many people are surprised to learn that the citizenship status of soldiers fighting in the U.S. armed forces is not always American. Some of the soldiers will earn the right to become citizens through their bravery in battle. On April 11, 2003, Eduardo Aguirre, the director of the new Bureau of Citizenship and Immigration Services, awarded citizenship to selected wounded immigrant marines from the war on Iraq.

Although specific immigration policies have undergone dramatic alterations in recent years, what inspires people to speak out on U.S. immigration remains the same: a sense of the importance of speaking out on an issue that continues to change.

Notes

1. Tom Brokaw, NBC Nightly News broadcast, March 25, 2003.

2. Francis Higginson, "A Short and True Description of New England," 1629. www.winthropsociety.org.

3. Jon Gjerde, ed., Major Problems in American Immigration and Ethnic History. New York: Houghton Mifflin, 1998, p. 1.

4. Report to a committee of the Common Council of the City of New York from the Almshouse Commissioner of New York City, January 20, 1847, in House Document No. 54, United States 29th Cong., 2nd sess., 1847, pp. 8–9.

5. Roger Daniels, *American Immigration: A Student Companion.* New York: Oxford University Press, 2001, p. 12.

6. Charles Ezra Clarke, agricultural address delivered to the Agricultural Society of Lewis County, New York, September 20, 1849.

7. Booker T. Washington, "An Address Delivered at the Opening of the Cotton States and the International Exhibition," Atlanta, Georgia, September 18, 1895, in Alice Moore Dunbar, ed., *Masterpieces of Negro Eloquence.* New York: G.K. Hall, 1997, p. 183.

8. Daniels, *American Immigration*, p. 14.

9. Bartolomeo Vanzetti, speech before Judge Webster Thayer, Dedham, Massachusetts, April 19, 1927, in Brian MacArthur, ed., *The Penguin Book of Twentieth-Century Speeches.* New York: Penguin Books, 1994, p. 100.

10. Dorothy Thompson, "Stopping Propaganda," speech delivered to the American Federation of Women's Clubs, May 9, 1939, in Calvin McLeod Logue, ed., *Representative American Speeches, 1937–1997.* New York: H.W. Wilson, 1997, p. 57.

11. Daniel K. Inouye, Senate debate, April 20, 1988, in James Ciment, ed., *Encyclopedia of American Immigration.* Vol. 4. Armonk, NY: M.E. Sharpe, 2001, p. 1416.

12. Hubert H. Humphrey, speech delivered to the U.S. Senate, May 16, 1952, in *Congressional Record*, 82nd Cong., 2nd sess., 1952, pp. 5319–22.

13. Steven A. Camarota, "The Impact of Immigration on California," *Immigration Review*, Summer 1998. www.cis.org.

14. Raul Yzaguirre, Mercy College commencement address, White Plains, New York, May 31, 1994, in Deborah G. Straub, ed., *Voices of Multicultural America: Notable Speeches Delivered by African, Asian, Hispanic, and Native Americans, 1790–1995.* Detroit: Gale Research, 1996, pp. 1329–30.

15. Ann Chih Lin, ed., *Immigration.* Washington, DC: CQ Press, 2002, p. ix.

CHAPTER
O N E

Voices of
American
Pluralists

Immigrants Deserve Public Assistance

Joseph Priestley

In 1794, British emigrant Joseph Priestley and his family fled religious persecution and settled in Philadelphia, Pennsylvania. Upon his arrival, Priestley, a natural scientist, joined a scholarly club that included such luminaries as Benjamin Franklin and Erasmus Darwin. In addition to his intellectual pursuits, Priestley was also a minister, and he established the first Unitarian church in America. His sermons were often attended by dignitaries such as Vice President John Adams.

In this 1797 sermon, Priestley appeals to his audience for the establishment and support of a public institution to serve the needs of recent immigrants. He argues that all Americans benefit when social accommodation and financial assistance are provided to liberty-seeking immigrants from around the world.

Now all of you who now hear me, may be expected to have this sympathy for strangers, and emigrants, in some degree; since, if not yourselves, yet your fathers, or not very remote ancestors, were also strangers, and not in a distant country, as Egypt was with respect to the Israelites, but in this very country in which we are now met. We should, therefore, behave to one another, in this land in which we may all be said to be equally strangers, as brethren; brethren, not merely as partaking of the same human nature, but brethren in affliction, difficulty and trials. . . .

Joseph Priestley, speech delivered to the Philadelphia Society for the Information and Assistance of Persons Emigrating from Foreign Countries, Philadelphia, PA, February 19, 1797.

That, in some way or other, many poor emigrants are entitled to assistance, will appear to every person who shall consider their situation.

Emigrants Are Hard Workers

It may be depended upon that, in general, emigrants are of the more industrious class of people. For the enterprizing, as the emigrants in some degree must be, are chiefly of that character. The indolent, as well as the timid, stay at home, content to starve, rather than make any attempt, that shall appear in the least degree hazardous, to better their condition. The weak and the sickly, the aged and infirm, however willing, cannot leave their country, and the friends on whom they depend. It is therefore probable that, with a little seasonable assistance, the poor emigrant, being disposed to industry, will soon be in a condition to provide for himself, and even to reimburse his benefactor.

It may be said that persons must be very thoughtless and improvident, to leave their country, though ever so poor, without a certainty of finding subsistence in another, and therefore that, on persons of so little foresight, money will be thrown away. This, no doubt, may be the case. But many, and we may well suppose, the greater part, of the necessitous and helpless persons, whose cause I am pleading, were only misinformed with respect to the country to which they have emigrated; and it is by no means easy, especially to persons in their low situation, to procure good information.

Those emigrants who had friends in this country will of course find employment with them, or assistance from them, and these are no objects of the present charity. But even some of these find their friends dead, or removed, or on some other account incapacitated to give them the assistance they had reason to expect. And many came without any friends at all, but with high expectations from such accounts as were given them of this country; as that they would meet with no difficulty, that if they were able and willing to labour, they could not fail to find employment, and that all labour would be abundantly rewarded. But many of these were manufacturers in their own country, and now find, to their great surprize, that their skill and industry are not wanted here, and can be of no service to them, and that there is no kind of labour, to which they have been accustomed, or to which they are equal, by which they can, at least can immediately, get a living.

Assistance and Encouragement

Also many emigrants have suffered extremely during the voyage. They are landed in a sickly condition, or soon become sickly by the change of climate; so that for a long time they are unable to do anything at all, and they find expenses at inns and lodging houses much greater than they had any idea of; so that the little money they might bring with them is soon expended, and they are left wholly destitute. In this case, if they meet with no relief from the charitable and well disposed, they must inevitably perish. Whereas, with a little assistance and encouragement, which is often of more real use than money, they may soon recover their health, strength, and spirits; and with proper advice with respect to the disposal of themselves, they may, in a short time, become useful citizens.

For, I would observe, that the benefit of this institution is not confined to giving pecuniary assistance to emigrants. Advice how to dispose of themselves to the most advantage, directions to cheap places of accommodation, some care to see that they are not imposed upon, and especially directions where to find employment, are often of much more use to them than money. . . . And if there was no public institution to which [the poor emigrant] could have recourse, conducted by persons qualified to give him the best advice, he would be reduced to the necessity of begging from door to door, and thereby become a nuisance, instead of a benefit, to society.

Hence then we see the use of a *public institution*, which being generally known, necessitous emigrants will of course be directed to it; and thus none of their time will be lost, or their money needlessly expended. But no institution of this kind can be supported without funds, as well as proper officers; and therefore this institution, the utility of which is so apparent, has a just claim to the benefactions of those who wish to employ what they can spare to the most advantage, for the service of their fellow creatures.

The present calamitous and oppressed state of Europe should more particularly draw the kind attention of the inhabitants of this country to the emigrants from that part of the world. Europe is not only overburdened with poor, but oppressed with servitude; so that the poor are not only unable to subsist by their labour, but lie under great restrictions with respect to civil and religious liberty. They are even, in a great measure, deprived of the satisfaction of expressing their feelings, of making complaints, or applying for redress of their grievances.

Many persons of better condition in those countries, especially in Great Britain and Ireland, unable to bear the encroachments that are continually making on their liberties, civil and religious, and despairing of doing any good by any exertions of theirs, are now coming hither, bringing with them very considerable capitals, by which this country is enriched. In consequence of the purchases that foreigners of various descriptions, and especially those of this class, who have the greatest confidence in this government, are making, the price of your lands is daily rising, and your labourers and artisans are getting higher wages. This circumstance adding much to the wealth of the country in general, you are better able, out of the emolument accruing to yourselves from European persecution, to assist those who are distressed in consequence of it. The poor emigrant, therefore, in fact, only asks of you some part of that which you have gained by his more opulent brethren. These more opulent emigrants will, no doubt, exert themselves in behalf of their distressed countrymen; but it is not reasonable that the whole of the burden should lie upon them. Many of them suffer considerably in their fortunes by the disadvantageous sale of their property in Europe, and the greater expense at which they are obliged to live here.

Let those, then, whose ancestors, if not themselves, were driven from Europe, by the same spirit of persecution which still prevails there, feel for those who are now in a similar situation; though it must be acknowledged, and with gratitude, that they now come with much better prospects. . . .

But some distressed emigrants, you will say, are men who

have fled from their creditors, perhaps from the justice of their country: Are these entitled to our assistance? I answer, that these cases cannot now be many, and it is not possible for us, at this distance, to distinguish them. Besides, the most vicious in one country, and especially a distant one, being separated from their former connexions, and entering into new ones, of a better cast, may become reformed and useful citizens. Our natures being the same, the greater advantage to which the best of us appear is owing chiefly to our education and connexions, for which we are indebted to a kind providence. Let us, then, show our gratitude to that providence which has favoured us, by our good will and liberality to those who, in this respect, as well as others, have been less favoured. Seasonable kindness may awaken the dormant seed of virtue, especially in a country like this, in which there are few temptations to vice. How many respectable, as well as opulent families in America, have arisen from the most indigent, and the most profligate in Europe. And this is so far from being the subject of reproach, that it is a just ground of praise.

The Strength of Democracy

Carl Schurz

Carl Schurz, the first German immigrant elected to the
U.S. Senate, served as President Abraham Lincoln's minister to Spain before resigning his post to become a major
general in the Union army during the Civil War. A journalist, political reformer, and master of public speaking in
both English and German, he wrote and delivered many
speeches on behalf of the Republican Party.

In this 1859 address delivered on the occasion of a
campaign stop in Massachusetts, Schurz frames the question of whether citizens of foreign birth should be made
to wait two years before being allowed to vote as an issue
of equal protection. He argues that the principle of equal
rights established by the Constitution is an essential ingredient in the success of the nation. He also asserts that
such representation is the key principle that differentiates
a democracy from ancient kingdoms and Old World
types of government.

A few days ago I stood on the cupola of your State-
house and overlooked for the first time this venera-
ble city and the country surrounding it. Then the
streets and hills and waters around me began to teem with
the life of historical recollections, recollections dear to all
mankind, and a feeling of pride arose in my heart, and I said
to myself, I, too, am an American citizen. There was Bunker
Hill; there Charlestown, Lexington, and Dorchester Heights

Carl Schurz, speech in Massachusetts, April 18, 1859.

not far off; there the harbor into which the British tea was sunk; there the place where the old liberty tree stood; there John Hancock's house; there Benjamin Franklin's birthplace. And now I stand in this grand old hall, which so often resounded with the noblest appeals that ever thrilled American hearts, and where I am almost afraid to hear the echo of my own feeble voice. Oh, sir, no man that loves liberty, wherever he may have first seen the light of day, can fail on this sacred spot to pay his tribute to Americanism. And here, with all these glorious memories crowding upon my heart, I will offer mine. I, born in a foreign land, pay my tribute to Americanism? Yes, for to me the word "Americanism," *true* "Americanism," comprehends the noblest ideas which ever swelled a human heart with noble pride.

Looking to America

It is one of the earliest recollections of my boyhood that one summer night our whole village was stirred up by an uncommon occurrence. I say our village, for I was born not far from that beautiful spot where the Rhine rolls his green waters out of the wonderful gate of the Seven Mountains and then meanders with majestic tranquillity through one of the most glorious valleys of the world. That night our neighbors were pressing around a few wagons covered with linen sheets and loaded with household utensils and boxes and trunks to their utmost capacity. One of our neighboring families was moving far away across a great water, and it was said that they would never again return. And I saw silent tears trickling down weather-beaten cheeks, and the hands of rough peasants firmly pressing each other, and some of the men and women hardly able to speak when they nodded to one another a last farewell. At last the train started into motion, they gave three cheers for *America*, and then in the first gray dawn of the morning I saw them wending their way over the hill until they disappeared in the shadow of the forest. And I heard many a man say how happy he would be if he could go with them to that great and free country where a man could be himself.

That was the first time that I heard of America, and my

childish imagination took possession of a land covered partly with majestic trees, partly with flowery prairies, immeasurable to the eye, and intersected with large rivers and broad lakes— a land where everybody could do what he thought best, and where nobody need be poor because everybody was free.

And later, when I was old enough to read, and descriptions of this country and books on American history fell into my hands, the offspring of my imagination acquired the colors of reality and I began to exercise my brain with the thought of what man might be and become when left perfectly free to himself. And still later, when ripening into manhood, I looked up from my school books into the stir and bustle of the world, and the trumpet tones of struggling humanity struck my ear and thrilled my heart, and I saw my nation shake her chains in order to burst them, and I heard a gigantic, universal shout for liberty rising up to the skies; and, at last, after having struggled manfully and drenched the earth of fatherland with the blood of thousands of noble beings, I saw that nation crushed down again, not only by overwhelming armies but by the deadweight of customs and institutions and notions and prejudices which past centuries had heaped upon them, and which a moment of enthusiasm, however sublime, could not destroy; then I consoled an almost despondent heart with the idea of a youthful people and of original institutions clearing the way for an untrammeled development of the ideal nature of man. Then I turned my eyes instinctively across the Atlantic Ocean; and America and Americanism, as I fancied them, appeared to me as the last depositories of the hopes of all true friends of humanity.

I say all this, not as though I indulged in the presumptuous delusion that my personal feelings and experience would be of any interest to you but in order to show you what America is to the thousands of thinking men in the Old World who, disappointed in their fondest hopes and depressed by the saddest experience, cling with their last remnant of confidence in human nature to the last spot on earth where man is free to follow the road to attainable perfection, and where, unbiased by the disastrous influence of traditional notions, customs, and institutions, he acts on his own responsibility. They ask themselves: Was it but a wild delusion when we thought that man has the faculty to be free and to govern himself? Have we been fighting, were we ready to die for a mere phantom, for a mere product of a morbid imagination? This question downtrodden humanity cries out into the world, and from this country it expects an answer.

As its advocate I speak to you. I will speak of Americanism as the great representative of the reformatory age, as the great champion of the dignity of human nature, as the great repository of the last hopes of suffering mankind. I will speak of the ideal mission of this country and of this people. . . .

Equals in the Eyes of the Law

The youthful elements which constitute people of the New World cannot submit to rules which are not of their own making; they must throw off the fetters which bind them to an old, decrepit order of things. They resolve to enter the great family of nations as an independent member. And in the colony of free humanity, whose mother country is the world, they establish *the republic of equal rights, where the title of manhood is the title to citizenship.* My friends, if I had a thousand tongues and a voice strong as the thunder of heaven, they would not be sufficient to impress upon your minds forcibly enough the greatness of this idea, the overshadowing glory of this result. This was the dream of the truest friends of man from the beginning; for this the noblest blood of martyrs has been shed; for this has mankind waded through seas of blood and tears. There it is now; there it stands, the noble fabric in all the splendor of reality.

They speak of the greatness of the Roman Republic! Oh, sir, if I could call the proudest of Romans from his grave, I would take him by the hand and say to him, Look at this picture, and at this! The greatness of thy Roman Republic consisted in its despotic rule over the world; the greatness of the American Republic consists in the secured right of man to govern himself. The dignity of the Roman citizen consisted in his exclusive privileges; the dignity of the American citizen consists in his holding the natural rights of his neighbor just as sacred as his own. The Roman Republic recognized and protected the *rights of the citizen*, at the same time disregarding and leaving unprotected the *rights of man;* Roman citizenship was founded upon monopoly, not upon the claims of human nature. What the citizen of Rome claimed for himself, he did not respect in others; his own greatness was his only object; his own liberty, as he regarded it, gave him the privilege to oppress his fellow beings. His democracy, instead of elevating mankind to his own level, trampled the rights of man into the dust. The security of the Roman Republic, therefore, consisted in the power of the sword; the security of the American Republic rests in the equality of human rights! The Roman Republic perished by the sword; the American Republic will stand as long as the equality of human rights remains inviolate. Which of the two republics is the greater—the republic of the Roman or the republic of *man?*

True Americanism

Sir, I wish the words of the Declaration of Independence, "that all men are created free and equal, and are endowed with certain inalienable rights," were inscribed upon every gatepost within the limits of this republic. From this principle the revolutionary fathers derived their claim to independence; upon this they founded the institutions of this country; and the whole structure was to be the living incarnation of this idea. This principle contains the program of our political existence. It is the most progressive and at the same time the most conservative one; the most progressive, for it takes even the lowliest members of the human family out of their degradation and inspires them with the elevating consciousness of equal human dignity; the most conservative, for it makes a common cause of individual rights. From the equality of rights springs identity of our highest interests; you cannot subvert your neighbor's rights without striking a dangerous blow at your own. And when the rights of one cannot be infringed without finding a ready defense in all others who defend their own rights in defending his, then and only then are the rights of all safe against the usurpations of governmental authority.

This general identity of interests is the only thing that can guarantee the stability of democratic institutions. Equality of rights, embodied in general self-government, is the great moral element of true democracy; it is the only reliable safety valve in the machinery of modern society. There is the solid foundation of our system of government; there is our mission; there is our greatness; there is our safety; there and nowhere else! This is true Americanism and to this I pay the tribute of my devotion. . . .

Specific Concerns About Immigrants

True, there are difficulties connected with an organization of society founded upon the basis of equal rights. Nobody denies it. A large number of those who come to you from foreign lands are not as capable of taking part in the administration of government as the man who was fortunate enough to drink the milk of liberty in his cradle. And certain religious denominations do, perhaps, nourish principles which are hardly in accordance with the doctrines of true democracy. There is a conglomeration on this continent of heterogeneous elements; there is a warfare of clashing interest and unruly aspirations; and, with all this, our democratic system gives rights to the ignorant and power to the inexperienced. And the billows of passion will lash the sides of the ship, and the storm of party warfare will bend its masts, and the pusillanimous will cry out—"Master, master, we perish!" But the genius of true democracy will arise from his slumber and rebuke the winds and the raging of the water, and say unto them—"Where is your faith?" Aye, where is the faith that led the fathers of this republic to invite the weary and burdened of all nations to the enjoyment of equal rights? Where is that broad and generous confidence in the efficiency of true democratic institutions? Has the present generation forgotten that true democracy bears in itself the remedy for all the difficulties that may grow out of it?

It is an old dodge of the advocates of despotism throughout the world that the people who are not experienced in self-government are not fit for the exercise of self-government and must first be educated under the rule of a superior authority. But at the same time the advocates of despotism will never offer them an opportunity to acquire experience in self-government lest they suddenly become fit for its independent exercise. To this treacherous sophistry the fathers of this republic proposed the noble doctrine that liberty is the best school for liberty, and that self-government cannot be learned but by practising it. This, sir, is a truly American idea; this is true Americanism; and to this I pay the tribute of my devotion.

You object that some people do not understand their own interests? There is nothing that, in the course of time, will make a man better understand his interests than the independent management of his own affairs on his own responsibility. You object that people are ignorant? There is no better schoolmaster in the world than self-government independently exercised. You object that people have no just idea of their duties as citizens? There is no other source from which they can derive a just notion of their duties than the enjoyment of the rights from which they arise. You object that people are misled by their religious prejudices and by the intrigues of the Roman hierarchy? Since when have the enlightened citizens of this republic lost their faith in the final invincibility of truth? Since when have they forgotten that if the Roman or any other church plants the seed of superstition, liberty sows broadcast the seed of enlightenment? Do they no longer believe in the invincible spirit of inquiry, which characterizes the reformatory age? If the struggle be fair, can the victory be doubtful?

As to religious fanaticism, it will prosper under oppression; it will feed on persecution; it will grow strong by proscription; but it is powerless against genuine democracy. It may indulge in short-lived freaks of passion or in wily intrigues, but it will die of itself, for its lungs are not adapted to breathe the atmosphere of liberty. It is like the shark of the sea: drag him into the air and the monster will perhaps struggle fearfully and frighten timid people with the powerful blows of his tail and the terrible array of his teeth; but leave him quietly to die and he will die. But engage with him in a hand-to-hand struggle even then, and the last of his convulsions may fatally punish your rash attempt. Against fanaticism, genuine democracy wields an irresistible weapon—it is *toleration*. Toleration will not strike down the fanatic but it will quietly and gently disarm him. But fight fanaticism *with* fanaticism and you will restore it to its own congenial element. . . .

Is it not wonderful how nations who have won their liberty by the severest struggles become so easily impatient of the small inconveniences and passing difficulties which are almost inseparably connected with the practical working of general self-government? How they so easily forget that rights may be abused and yet remain inalienable rights? Europe has witnessed many an attempt for the establishment of democratic institutions; some of them were at first successful and the people were free, but the abuses and inconveniences connected with liberty became at once apparent. Then the ruling classes of society, in order to get rid of the abuses, restricted liberty; they did, indeed, get rid of the abuses but they got rid of liberty at the same time. You heard liberal governments there speak of protecting and regulating the liberty of the press; and in order to prevent that liberty from being abused they adopted measures, apparently harmless at first, which ultimately resulted in an absolute censorship. Would it be much better if we, recognizing the right of man to the exercise of self-government, should, in order to protect the purity of the ballot box, restrict the right of suffrage? . . .

Democracy and the Right to Vote Are Inseparable

A violation of equal rights can never serve to maintain institutions which are founded upon equal rights. A contrary policy is not only pusillanimous and small but it is senseless. It reminds me of the soldier who, for fear of being shot in battle, committed suicide on the march; or of the man who would cut off his foot because he had a corn on his toe. It is that ridiculous policy of premature despair which commences to throw the freight overboard when there is a suspicious cloud in the sky. . . .

I invite you, I entreat you, I conjure you, come one and all, and make our prairies resound and our forests shake and our ears ring and tingle with your appeals for the equal rights of man. . . .

These are the ideas which have rallied around the banner of liberty, not only the natives of the soil but an innumerable host of Germans, Scandinavians, Scotchmen, Frenchmen, and a goodly number of Irishmen, also. And here I tell you, those are mistaken who believe that the Irish heart is devoid of those noble impulses which will lead him to the side of justice, where he sees his own rights respected and unendangered.

Under this banner all the languages of civilized mankind are spoken, every creed is protected, every right is sacred. There stands every element of Western society, with enthusiasm for a great cause, with confidence in each other, with honor to themselves. This is the banner floating over the glorious valley which stretches from the western slope of the Alleghenies to the Rocky Mountains—that Valley of Jehoshaphat where the nations of the world assemble to celebrate the resurrection of human freedom. The inscription on that banner is not "Opposition to the Democratic Party for the sake of placing a new set of men into office"; for this battle cry of speculators our hearts have no response. Nor is it "restriction of slavery and restriction of the right of suffrage," for this—believe my words, I entreat you—this would be the signal of deserved, inevitable, and disgraceful defeat. But the inscription is "Liberty and equal rights, common to all as the air of heaven—liberty and equal rights, one and inseparable!"

With this banner we stand before the world. In this sign—in this sign alone, and no other—there is victory. And thus, sir, we mean to realize the great cosmopolitan idea upon which the existence of the American nation rests. Thus we mean to fulfill the great mission of true Americanism, thus we mean to answer the anxious question of downtrodden humanity: "Has *man* the faculty to be free and to govern himself?" The answer is a triumphant "Aye," thundering into the ears of the despots of the Old World that "a man is a man for all that"; proclaiming to the oppressed that they are held in subjection on false pretenses; cheering the hearts of the despondent friends of man with consolation and renewed confidence.

This is true Americanism, clasping mankind to its great heart. Under its banner we march; let the world follow.

Immigration Quotas Are Un-American

Robert H. Clancy

Immigration quotas established by Congress in 1921 were set at 3 percent of the 1910 census population of a given nationality already in the United States. The bill that later became the Johnson-Reed Act of 1924 restricted these numbers even further. Robert H. Clancy, a four-term congressman from Detroit, Michigan, argued against these quotas and the passage of the Johnson-Reed Act. In this speech before Congress, Clancy insists that the majority of immigrants in Detroit, for example, are moral, industrious residents who contribute to the city's prosperity. Clancy argues that restrictive immigration quotas antagonize racial hatred and stultify true American principles of freedom and democracy.

Since the foundations of the American commonwealth were laid in colonial times over 300 years ago, vigorous complaint and more or less bitter persecution have been aimed at newcomers to our shores. Also the congressional reports of about 1840 are full of abuse of English, Scotch, Welsh immigrants as paupers, criminals, and so forth.

Old citizens in Detroit of Irish and German descent have told me of the fierce tirades and propaganda directed against the great waves of Irish and Germans who came over from 1840 on for a few decades to escape civil, racial, and religious persecution in their native lands.

The "Know-Nothings," lineal ancestors of the Ku-Klux

Robert H. Clancy, speech before the United States Congress, April 8, 1924.

Klan, bitterly denounced the Irish and Germans as mongrels, scum, foreigners, and a menace to our institutions, much as other great branches of the Caucasian race of glorious history and antecedents are berated to-day. All are riff-raff, unassimilables, "foreign devils," swine not fit to associate with the great chosen people—a form of national pride and hallucination as old as the division of races and nations.

But to-day it is the Italians, Spanish, Poles, Jews, Greeks, Russians, Balkanians, and so forth, who are the racial lepers. And it is eminently fitting and proper that so many Members of this House with names as Irish as Paddy's pig, are taking the floor these days to attack once more as their kind has attacked for seven bloody centuries the fearful fallacy of chosen peoples and inferior peoples. The fearful fallacy is that one is made to rule and the other to be abominated. . . .

Contributions of Immigrants in Detroit

In this bill we find racial discrimination at its worst—a deliberate attempt to go back 84 years in our census taken every 10 years so that a blow may be aimed at peoples of eastern and southern Europe, particularly at our recent allies in the Great War—Poland and Italy.

Of course the Jews too are aimed at, not directly, because they have no country in Europe they can call their own, but they are set down among the inferior peoples. Much of the animus against Poland and Russia, old and new, with the countries that have arisen from the ruins of the dead Czar's European dominions, is directed against the Jew.

We have many American citizens of Jewish descent in Detroit, tens of thousands of them—active in every profession and every walk of life. They are particularly active in charities and merchandising. One of our greatest judges, if not the greatest, is a Jew. Surely no fair-minded person with a knowledge of the facts can say the Jews of Detroit are a menace to the city's or the country's well-being. . . .

Forty or fifty thousand Italian-Americans live in my district in Detroit. They are found in all walks and classes of life—common hard labor, the trades, business, law, medicine, dentistry, art, literature, banking, and so forth.

They rapidly become Americanized, build homes, and make themselves into good citizens. They brought hardihood, physique, hope, and good humor with them from their outdoor life in Sunny Italy, and they bear up under the terrific strain of life and work in busy Detroit.

One finds them by thousands digging streets, sewers, and building foundations, and in the automobile and iron and steel fabric factories of various sorts. They do the hard work that the native-born American dislikes. Rapidly they rise in life and join the so-called middle and upper classes. . . .

The Italian-Americans of Detroit played a glorious part in the Great War. They showed themselves as patriotic as the native born in offering the supreme sacrifice.

In all, I am informed, over 300,000 Italian-speaking soldiers enlisted in the American Army, almost 10 percent of our total fighting force. Italians formed about 4 percent of the population of the United States and they formed 10 per-

Newly arrived immigrants wait in the immigration building on Ellis Island, New York.

cent of the American military force. Their casualties were 12 percent. . . .

I wish to take the liberty of informing the House that from my personal knowledge and observation of tens of thousands of Polish-Americans living in my district in Detroit that their Americanism and patriotism are unassailable from any fair or just standpoint.

The Polish-Americans are as industrious and as frugal and as loyal to our institutions as any class of people who have come to the shores of this country in the past 300 years. They are essentially home builders, and they have come to this country to stay. They learn the English language as quickly as possible, and take pride in the rapidity with which they become assimilated and adopt our institutions.

Figures available to all show that in Detroit in the World War the proportion of American volunteers of Polish blood was greater than the proportion of Americans of any other racial descent. . . .

Polish-Americans do not merit slander nor defamation. If not granted charitable or sympathetic judgment, they are at least entitled to justice and to the high place they have won in American and European history and citizenship.

The force behind the Johnson bill and some of its champions in Congress charge that opposition to the racial discrimination feature of the 1800 quota basis arises from "foreign blocs." They would give the impression that 100 percent Americans are for it and that the sympathies of its opponents are of the "foreign-bloc" variety, and bear stigma of being "hyphenates." I meet that challenge willingly. I feel my Americanism will stand any test.

The So-Called Hyphenated Americans

The foreign born of my district writhe under the charge of being called "hyphenates." The people of my own family were all hyphenates—English-Americans, German-Americans, Irish-Americans. They began to come in the first ship or so after the *Mayflower*. But they did not come too early to miss the charge of anti-Americanism. Roger Williams was driven out of the Puritan colony of Salem to die in the wilderness because he objected "violently" to blue laws and the burning or hanging of rheumatic old women on witchcraft charges. He would not "assimilate" and was "a grave menace to American Institutions and democratic government."

My family put 11 men and boys into the Revolutionary War, and I am sure they and their women and children did not suffer so bitterly and sacrifice until it hurt to establish the autocracy of bigotry and intolerance which exists in many quarters to-day in this country. Some of these men and boys shed their blood and left their bodies to rot on American battle fields. To me real Americanism and the American flag are the product of the blood of men and of the tears of women and children of a different type than the rampant "Americanizers" of to-day. . . .

It must never be forgotten also that the Johnson bill, although it claims to favor the northern and western European peoples only, does so on a basis of comparison with the southern and western European peoples. The Johnson bill cuts down materially the number of immigrants allowed to come from northern and western Europe, the so-called Nordic peoples. . . .

Then I would be true to the principles for which my forefathers fought and true to the real spirit of the magnificent United States of to-day. I can not stultify myself by voting for the present bill and overwhelm my country with racial hatreds and racial lines and antagonisms drawn even tighter than they are to-day.

The Historical Contributions of America's Immigrants

Harold Fields

Immigration policy of the 1930s reflected the ongoing economic crisis in the United States, exacerbating the fear that immigrants were taking jobs away from native workers. The government began deliberations on the question of accepting refugees during this swell of "nativist" rhetoric. Consequently, the latest wave of immigrants faced recently imposed restrictions such as the 1924 quota system that limited the number of foreigners allowed entrance to the country.

Concerns that immigration would alter the racial composition of Anglo-American society also factored into the immigration debate. Advocates of pluralism such as advertising executive Harold Fields felt the need to denounce such racist arguments. In this nationally broadcast address from January 1937, Fields reminds the audience of the historical contributions immigrants have made to American life. Fields was well versed in the immigration debate as he served as chairman for various social justice organizations, several of which dealt with immigration and citizenship.

Harold Fields, speech broadcast from National Broadcasting Studios, New York, NY, January 1937.

"**D**ifferent periods, different prejudices" once said an eminent historian. That is particularly true today when "Lo, the poor Indian" has given away to "Lo, the poor alien." For today it is the alien who is made the target of all charges. If he is working, we say he is taking employment away from Americans; if he is not working, we condemn him for being a charge upon relief. If he is wealthy, we criticize him for exploiting our country; if he is poor we vilify him for causing us to support him. We cause his name to be considered as synonymous with crime and illiteracy and undesirabilities and anti-social policies. He is the communist, the atheist, the anarchist, the libertine, and the instigator for everything that means license in morals, ethics, conduct of living, and standards.

When we charge the alien with having nurtured communism in this country, we do so in ignorance, or with our tongue in our cheek. For anyone truly desirous of learning the facts will learn from our Department of Labor and the Department of Justice—both United States Government bodies—that the leaders and spokesmen of communism are native-born Americans.

When we charge the alien with the high degree of racketeering and crime, we turn our faces away from the findings of the federal commissions headed by such patriotic fearless Americans as the late Attorney-General George W. Wickersham. It was his commission that statistically and impartially proved that there was a greater percentage of native-born criminals in our jails than in our population, and that the percentage of the foreign-born criminals was less than their ratio to Americans.

One national weekly set out to prove that there were millions of aliens on relief, costing the citizens millions of dollars a week. The demand for proof was overwhelming; no proof was forthcoming. The statistics were shown to be the figments of the imagination of the author; so they right-about-faced, and set up the countercharge that millions of aliens were indeed at work, taking away millions of jobs from citizens who were thus left unemployed. Obviously if the first statement was true, the second was false; if the second was true, the first was false. And since neither was proved, I leave it to your decision as to which, if either, was true.

Who is this poor alien whom we are baiting so mercilessly? He is the Englishman, the Swede, the German, the Frenchman, the Jew, the Italian, and countless others. He and his kind have been coming here for over one hundred fifty years, contributing to our welfare, our culture, our wealth. We are apt to forget that.

The intimate records of history tell of the thousands of unnamed Italians, Irish, Poles, and Norwegians who cleared forests to prepare the land for the railroad tracks that were to follow. Our highways go from the rising sun to the setting sun across what once had been swamp and desert and plain—and all through the long-working, cheaply paid labor of the thousands of foreigners. Our ditches were dug by the sweat of their hands and the gnawing pain in their backs. Our pipe lines were laid in ditches that these aliens had dug. Our buildings rose, story above story, as foreigners toiled to give material form to our wealth. And if we want to be honest with ourselves, for all this wealth that they helped to create, we did not give them wealth.

Because we Americans exploited them, anti-contract-labor clauses were written into our immigration laws by our own fellow Americans. Because they received such a pittance, American labor organized strikes. Because they were subjected to the vilest conditions of work and servitude, to the lowest pay, to the deepest violations of decency in hours of work and types of factories—because of these conditions, Americans passed labor laws correcting conditions that American industry was responsible for and was taking advantage of. For every dollar they received, they gave five and ten dollars worth of labor and wealth. We needed them, we used them, and now that machinery has taken so many of their places, we abuse them.

Immigrants Who Have Changed American Life

And yet they have given us a splendid heritage of wealth and contribution. Alexander Hamilton, an immigrant from the West Indies, set our financial structure to rights, kept our country strong as he worked by the side of Washington, and helped to maintain our dignity and earnestness of purpose. From Switzerland came Albert Gallatin, who was Secretary of the Treasury under Jefferson. Carl Schurz left Germany and later proved to be one of the inspiring leaders in Lincoln's cabinet. Franklin K. Lane set out from Canada and enriched our worth through his vision and understanding as Secretary of the Interior. It was recently shown, in "Who's Who in America," that immigrants from the British Isles have become our outstanding clergymen, from France have come sculptors, from Switzerland have come educators, from Germany have come important business men and bankers, from Russia and Hungary and Italy have come artists and musicians. The list is so interminable that it becomes overwhelming. . . .

Among our artists have loomed Jonas Lie of Norway and Augustus St. Gaudens of France and Karl Bitter of Austria and John Muir of Scotland. How can our naturalists repay Switzerland for Louis Agassiz? Or our scientists repay Scotland for Alexander Bell? . . .

We delve into America's social problems through the writings of Jacob Riis of Denmark or Mary Antin of Jewish ancestry.

And what a wealth we owe for the eradication of disease to Doctor Alexis Carrel of France and Doctor William Osler of Canada and Doctor Abraham Jacobi of Germany and Doctor Gregory of Armenia.

Justices of courts, members of cabinets, congressmen, senators, mayors, musicians, editors, artists, business men, educators, saviors of our nation during times of war—these have often come to us as aliens. . . . Beside these, toward peace, there stride such churchmen as Stephen S. Wise of Hungary, and Archbishop John Ireland of Ireland, and Doctor Steiner of Austria, and Bishop Rihbany of Syria, and Evangeline Booth and Bishop Manning of England. These all are our supporters and our citizens, and these are the people who among others represent our aliens.

Behind a list altogether too long to detail looms a long plodding army of tens of millions who came to this country to develop our soil and cultivate our land, to increase our trade and develop our commerce, to enter professions and to further our arts, to fill the labor wants for skilled and unskilled work, to sweat and toil so that they and we might give happier lives to children born in this country.

And for all this we now condemn them and hiss them and sneer. As a means of evidencing that spirit of disfavor and intolerant approach, the alien in this country has been subjected to all sorts of discriminations.

If he is of the more intellectual group, and seeks to put his education to use by making a place for himself among the professions, he will find innumerable laws in all of the forty-eight states that will bar him from taking such a step. If he is skilled or unskilled in his labor qualifications, he will face the fact that more than four out of every five jobs are denied him by industry, that almost four out of every five memberships in labor unions are closed to him, and that every state in the Union has diversified laws on its statute books preventing him from engaging in remunerative work.

Unhappy Heritage of the Alien

He is blamed for being an alien even though we have, under no compulsion at all, freely admitted him to this country and, in many cases, passed laws, or refused to amend laws, that will keep him in that state of alienage for all time. We have thousands of foreign-born in this country who are not deportable and who cannot become naturalized. We can't send them out and we won't take them in. They are husbands of American-born girls, fathers of American-born children, heads of American establishments, and employers of American labor. They pay wages, taxes, and bills—but they remain stateless and are condemned for that statelessness, which we ourselves impose on them.

I have presented this story of what I call the unhappy heritage of the alien in lectures, in talks, in the press, and in publications. Again and again I find myself facing the persistently recurrent question: "Well, why do these foreign-born persist in remaining aliens? Why don't they show their interest in this country if they chose to come here by becoming citizens?" In one form or another that question is put—and it is a fair question—provided we are willing to face it fairly. Let's see what the answer is.

There are 4,500,000 aliens in this country today. They are the foreign-born who are legally resident in the United States and who in due time are entitled to naturalization. One million, five hundred thousand of them have already taken out their first papers. That leaves 3,000,000 aliens. A half million either are under age or haven't been here the required length of time. That leaves 2,500,000 aliens. About a quarter of a million have either applied for second papers or are utterly disqualified to apply because of our laws.

That leaves close to 2,000,000 aliens to be accounted for. This group is covered by those aliens who are just beginning to earn enough money to pay for their papers or whose interests in Americanization are being reawakened with economic recovery. They are flocking back to our night schools and joining our Works Progress Administration (WPA) forums. Take the number of aliens who have come to the National League for American Citizenship for naturalization aid in the past few years and note the relation to industrial conditions. In 1928 some 24,000 were helped; in 1929 about 30,000; in 1930 also 30,000; in 1931 some 26,000; in 1932 again 30,000; in 1933 about 28,000; in 1934 about 29,000; in 1935 some 31,000; and in 1936, approximately 34,000 aliens started on the road to becoming Americanized.

Immigration has now become a trickle; only about 36,000 are coming in annually. For every one that comes in, one goes out—emigrating from this land for permanent residence abroad. A sense of decency and good taste should then urge a campaign of good-will, of appreciation, to the end that this small residue might become eager to be Americanized.

For while we spend our time in disparaging the aliens, we overlook the more serious problem of creating an American citizenry as closely knit as that enjoyed by our English friends. We cannot do that by raising fears or contempt or by advocating intolerance on the part of any section or group of our people. A homogeneous America can become evolved only by making all residents of the United States, native-born or foreign-born alike, work together toward our common welfare.

My Fellow Immigrants

Franklin D. Roosevelt

President Franklin D. Roosevelt holds the distinction of
being the only man ever elected president four times.
Prior to his presidency Roosevelt had served many terms
in public office, including as secretary of the navy and
governor of New York. During his tenure as president,
the country suffered through such monumental crises as
the Great Depression and World War II. Roosevelt's leadership, calming manner, pleasant speaking voice, and
spirited wit endeared him to most of his constituency in
those trying times.

On the occasion of this 1938 speech, however, Roosevelt's audience, the conservative Daughters of the American Revolution (DAR), did not support the majority of
the president's social programs. The DAR was an organization of descendants of those men who helped achieve
American independence. They viewed the waves of immigrants in the late nineteenth and early twentieth centuries
as a threat to the purity of well-born heritage that descended from the Founding Fathers. In his "off-the-cuff"
speech Roosevelt reminds the DAR that all Americans are
descendants of "immigrants and revolutionists."

I couldn't let a fifth year go by without coming to see you.
I must ask you to take me just as I am, in a business suit—
and I see you are still in favor of national defense—take
me as I am, with no prepared remarks. You know, as a mat-

Franklin D. Roosevelt, speech delivered to the Daughters of the American Revolution, April 21, 1938.

ter of fact, I would have been here to one of your conventions in prior years—one or more—but it is not the time that it takes to come before you and speak for half an hour, it is the preparation for that half hour.

And I suppose that for every half-hour speech that I make before a convention or over the radio, I put in ten hours preparing it.

So I have to ask you to bear with me, to let me just come here without preparation to tell you how glad I am to avail myself of this opportunity, to tell you how proud I am, as a revolutionary descendant, to greet you.

I thought of preaching on a text, but I shall not. I shall only give you the text, and I shall not preach on it. I think I can afford to give you the text because it so

Franklin D. Roosevelt

happens, through no fault of my own, that I am descended from a number of people who came over in the *Mayflower*. More than that, every one of my ancestors on both sides— and when you go back four generations or five generations it means thirty-two or sixty-four of them—every single one of them, without exception, was in this land in 1776. And there was only one Tory among them.

The text is this: remember, remember always that all of us, and you and I especially, are descended from immigrants and revolutionists.

I am particularly glad to know that today you are making this fine appeal to the youth of America. To these rising generations, to our sons and grandsons and great-grandsons, we cannot overestimate the importance of what we are doing in this year, in our own generation, to keep alive the spirit of American democracy. The spirit of opportunity is the kind of spirit that has led us as a nation—not as a small group but as a nation—to meet the very great problems of the past.

We look for a younger generation that is going to be more American than we are. We are doing the best that we can, and yet we can do better than that, we can do more than that, by inculcating in the boys and girls of this country to-day some of the underlying fundamentals, the reasons that brought our immigrant ancestors to this country, the reasons that impelled our revolutionary ancestors to throw off a fascist yoke.

We have a great many things to do. Among other things in this world is the need of being very, very certain, no matter what happens, that the sovereignty of the United States will never be impaired.

There have been former occasions, conventions of the Daughters of the American Revolution, when voices were raised, needed to be raised, for better national defense. This year, you are raising those same voices and I am glad of it. But I am glad also that the government of the United States can assure you today that it is taking definite, practical steps for the defense of the nation.

Eliminating Nationality Quotas

John F. Kennedy

John F. Kennedy, the first Roman Catholic to be elected president, embraced his Irish ancestry. It followed that immigration reform became a matter of personal importance to him throughout his career. Among his other accomplishments, the Massachusetts-born Harvard graduate served with distinction in the navy and authored the Pulitzer Prize–winning *Profiles in Courage*. His final work, *A Nation of Immigrants*, relates through photographs and essays the histories of peoples who immigrated to America. In its pages, he also discusses the divergent and complex reasons émigrés have for leaving their home countries.

In this address presented to Congress just four months before his assassination in 1963, President Kennedy outlines his proposal to end the quota system created by the 1924 National Origins Act in which immigration from Northern Europe was favored over immigration from other parts of the world. Kennedy's vision of a liberalized immigration policy was realized when his successor, Lyndon Johnson, signed the Immigration and Nationality Act amendments in 1965.

I am transmitting herewith, for the consideration of the Congress, legislation revising and modernizing our immigration laws. More than a decade has elapsed since the last substantial amendment to these laws. I believe there ex-

---

John F. Kennedy, address to the United States Congress, July 23, 1963.

ists a compelling need for the Congress to re-examine and make certain changes in these laws.

The most urgent and fundamental reform I am recommending relates to the national origins system of selecting immigrants. Since 1924 it has been used to determine the number of quota immigrants permitted to enter the United States each year. Accordingly, although the legislation I am transmitting deals with many problems which require remedial action, it concentrates attention primarily upon revision of our quota immigration system. The enactment of this legislation will not resolve all of our important problems in the field of immigration law. It will, however, provide a sound basis upon which we can build in developing an immigration law that serves the national interest and reflects in every detail the principles of equality and human dignity to which our nation subscribes.

An End to Discriminatory Quotas

Present legislation establishes a system of annual quotas to govern immigration from each country. Under this system, 156,700 quota immigrants are permitted to enter the United States each year. The system is based upon the national origins of the population of the United States in 1920. The use of the year 1920 is arbitrary. It rests upon the fact that this system was introduced in 1924 and the last prior census was in 1920. The use of a national origins system is without basis in either logic or reason. It neither satisfies a national need nor accomplishes an international purpose. In an age of interdependence among nations, such a system is an anachronism, for it discriminates among applicants for admission into the United States on the basis of accident of birth.

Because of the composition of our population in 1920, the system is heavily weighted in favor of immigration from northern Europe and severely limits immigration from southern and eastern Europe and from other parts of the world. An American citizen with a Greek father or mother must wait at least eighteen months to bring his parents here to join him. A citizen whose married son or daughter, or brother or sister, is Italian cannot obtain a quota number for an even longer time. Meanwhile, many thousands of quota numbers are wasted because they are not wanted or needed by nationals of the countries to which they are assigned.

I recommend that there be substituted for the national origins system a formula governing immigration to the United States which takes into account (1) the skills of the immigrant and their relationship to our need; (2) the family relationship between immigrants and persons already here, so that the reuniting of families is encouraged and (3) the priority of registration. Present law grants a preference to immigrants with special skills, education or training. It also grants a preference to various relatives of United States citizens and lawfully resident aliens. But it does so only within a national origins quota. It should be modified so that those with the greatest ability to add to the national welfare, no matter where they were born, are granted the highest priority. The next priority should go to those who seek to be reunited with their relatives. As between applicants with equal claims the earliest registrant should be the first admitted.

Many problems of fairness and foreign policy are involved in replacing a system so long entrenched. The national origins system has produced large backlogs of applications in some countries, and too rapid a change might, in a system of limited immigration, so drastically curtail immigration in some countries the only effect might be to shift the unfairness from one group of nations to another. A reasonable time to adjust to any new system must be provided if individual hardships upon persons who were relying on the present system are to be avoided. In addition, any new system must have sufficient flexibility to allow adjustments to be made when it appears that immigrants from nations closely allied to the United States will be unduly restricted in their freedom to furnish the new seed population that has so long been a source of strength to our nation. . . .

Essential Quota Modifications

It is not alone the initial assignment of quota numbers which is arbitrary and unjust; additional inequity results from the failure of the law to permit full utilization of the authorized quota numbers. While American citizens wait for years for their relatives to receive a quota, approximately sixty thousand quota numbers are wasted each year because the countries to which they are assigned have far more numbers allocated to them than they have emigrants seeking to move to the United States. There is no way at present in which these numbers can be reassigned to nations where immense backlogs of applicants for admission to the United States have accumulated. I recommend that this deficiency in the law be corrected.

A special discriminatory formula is now used to regulate the immigration of persons who are attributable by their ancestry to an area called the Asia-Pacific triangle. This area embraces all countries from Pakistan to Japan and the Pacific islands north of Australia and New Zealand. Usually, the quota under which a prospective immigrant must enter is determined by his place of birth. However, if as much as one-half of an immigrant's ancestors came from nations in the Asia-Pacific triangle, he must rely upon the small quota assigned to the country of his ancestry, regardless of where he was born. This provision of our law should be repealed.

Other Changes

In order to remove other existing barriers to the reuniting of families, I recommend two additional improvements in the law.

First, parents of American citizens, who now have a preferred quota status, should be accorded nonquota status.

Second, parents of aliens resident in the United States, who now have no preference, should be accorded a preference, after skilled specialists and other relatives of citizens and alien residents.

These changes will have little effect on the number of immigrants admitted. They will have a major effect upon the individual hardships many of our citizens and residents now face in being separated from their parents.

In addition, I recommend the following changes in the law in order to correct certain deficiencies and improve its general application.

1. *Changes in the Preference Structure.* At present, the

procedure under which specially skilled or trained workers are permitted to enter this country too often prevents talented people from applying for visas to enter the United States. It often deprives us of immigrants who would be helpful to our economy and our culture. This procedure should be liberalized so that highly trained or skilled persons may obtain a preference without requiring that they secure employment here before emigrating. In addition, I recommend that a special preference be accorded workers with lesser skills who can fill specific needs in short supply in this country.

2. *Nonquota status for natives of Jamaica, Trinidad and Tobago should be granted.* Under existing law, no numerical limitation is imposed upon the number of immigrants coming from Canada, Mexico, Cuba, Haiti, the Dominican Republic, the Canal Zone or any independent country in Central or South America. But the language of the statute restricts this privilege to persons born in countries in the Caribbean area which gained their independence prior to the date of the last major amendment to the immigration and nationality statutes, in 1952. This accidental discrimination against the newly independent nations of the Western Hemisphere should be corrected.

3. *Persons afflicted with mental health problems should be admitted provided certain standards are met.* Today, any person afflicted with a mental disease or mental defect, psychotic personality, or epilepsy, and any person who has suffered an attack of mental illness, can enter this country only if a private bill is enacted for his benefit. Families which are able and willing to care for a mentally ill child or parent are often forced to choose between living in the United States and leaving their loved ones behind and not living in the United States but being able to see and care for their loved ones. Mental illness is not incurable. It should be treated like other illnesses. I recommend that the Attorney General, at his discretion and under proper safeguards, be authorized to waive those provisions of the law which prohibit the admission to the United States of persons with mental problems when they are close relatives of United States citizens and lawfully resident aliens. . . .

As I have already indicated the measures I have outlined

will not solve all the problems of immigration. Many of them will require additional legislation; some cannot be solved by any one country. But the legislation I am submitting will insure that progress will continue to be made toward our ideals and toward the realization of humanitarian objectives. The measures I have recommended will help eliminate discrimination between peoples and nations on a basis that is unrelated to any contribution that immigrants can make and is inconsistent with our traditions of welcome. Our investment in new citizens has always been a valuable source of our strength.

CHAPTER
T W O

Voices Opposed to Increased or Unregulated Immigration

Immigration Threatens the Nation's Political Structure

Garrett Davis

In December 1849, Garrett Davis, a unionist Democratic congressman and senator from Kentucky, was involved with the effort to revise the state's constitution. Davis felt that the framers of the U.S. Constitution had erred by not restricting immigration, and he hoped to incorporate strict anti-immigration language into Kentucky law. In this speech delivered at the constitutional convention in that year, Davis pleads his case. He predicts a catastrophic collapse of the U.S. political system unless swift action is taken to halt immigration, and concludes that without immigration restrictions, wars of race and religion are inevitable.

B ut why am I opposed to the encouragement of foreign immigration into our country, and disposed to apply any proper checks to it? Why do I propose to suspend to the foreigner, for twenty-one years after he shall have signified formally his intention to become a citizen of the United States, the right of suffrage, the birthright of no man but one native-born? It is because the mighty tides of immigration, each succeeding one increasing in volume, bring to us not only different languages, opinions, customs, and principles,

---

Garrett Davis, speech delivered before the Convention to Revise the Constitution of Kentucky, Frankfort, KY, December 17, 1849.

but hostile races, religions, and interests, and the traditionary prejudices of generations with a large amount of the turbulence, disorganizing theories, pauperism, and demoralization of Europe in her redundant population thrown upon us. This multiform and dangerous evil exists and will continue, for "the cry is, Still they come!" Large numbers in a short time, a few months or weeks, after getting into the country, and very many before they have remained the full time of probation, fall into the hands of demagogues and unscrupulous managers of elections, and by the commission of perjury and other crimes are made to usurp against law a portion of the political sovereignty of the country. They are ignorant of our institutions and the principles upon which they are founded; of the great interests of the country, and the questions of policy which divide our people; of the candidates for office, and their capacities, views, fitness, and former course of life. Instead of being qualified to aid in the great and difficult business of upholding the most complicated structure of government that ever had existence, and of successfully administering it for the good and happiness of the people and its own perpetuation, they constitute an uninformed, unreasoning, and, to a great extent, immoral power, wielded almost universally by desperate and profligate men who by this agency become enabled to carry into success their own bold, mercenary, and pernicious purposes; and to defeat those which the wise and the good devise for the benefit of the country and the preservation of constitutional liberty.

A Threat to Government Sovereignty

We cannot, with any safety, continue to admit with such lavish liberality those ever coming and ever increasing masses of immigrants into full political partnership and share with them the sovereignty of government. We are taught this truth no less by nature and reason than by fact and experience. . . . The most of those European immigrants, having been born and having lived in the ignorance and degradation of despotisms, without mental or moral culture, with but a vague consciousness of human rights, and no knowledge whatever of the principles of popular constitutional government, their interference in the political administration of our affairs, even when honestly intended, would be about as successful as that of the Indian in the arts and business of civilized private life; and when misdirected, as it would generally be, by bad and designing men, could be productive only of mischief, and from their numbers, of mighty mischief. The system inevitably and in the end will fatally depreciate, degrade, and demoralize the power which governs and rules our destinies.

I freely acknowledge that among such masses of immigrants there are men of noble intellect, of high cultivation, and of great moral worth; men every way adequate to the difficult task of free, popular, and constitutional government. But the number is lamentably small. There can be no contradistinction between them and the incompetent and vicious; and their admission would give no proper compensation, no adequate security against the latter if they, too, were allowed to share political sovereignty. . . .

A Political Solution Is Required

The question is, Shall they come and take possession of our country and our government, and rule us, or will we, who have the right, rule them and ourselves? I go openly, manfully, and perseveringly for the latter rule, and if it cannot be successfully asserted in all the United States, I am for taking measures to maintain it in Kentucky, and while we can. Now is the time—prevention is easier than cure. . . .

Washington and Jefferson and their associates, though among the wisest and most far-seeing of mankind, could not but descry in the future many formidable difficulties and dangers, and thus be premonished to provide against them in fashioning our institutions. If they had foreseen the vast, the appalling increase of immigration upon us at the present, there can be no reasonable doubt that laws to naturalize the foreigners and to give up to them the country, its liberties, its destiny, would not have been authorized by the constitution. The danger, though great, is not wholly without remedy. We can do something if we do it quickly. The German and Slavonic races are combining in the state of New York to elect candidates of their own blood to Congress. This is the beginning of the conflict of races on a large scale, and it must, in the nature of things, continue and increase. It must be universal and severe in all the field of labor, between the native and the stranger, and from the myriads of foreign laborers coming to us, if it does not become a contest for bread and subsistence, wages will at least be brought down so low as to hold our native laborers and their families in hopeless poverty. They cannot adopt the habits of life and live upon the stinted meager supplies to which the foreigner will restrict himself, and which is bounteous plenty to what he has been accustomed in the old country. Already these results are taking place in many of the mechanic arts. Duty, patriotism, and wisdom all require us to protect the labor, and to keep up to a fair scale the wages of our native-born people as far as by laws and measures of public policy it can be done.

The Dangers of Political Sovereignty

The foreigner, too, is the natural foe of the slavery of our state. He is opposed to it by all his past associations, and when he comes to our state he sees 200,000 laborers of a totally different race to himself excluding him measurably from employment and wages. He hears a measure agitated to send these 200,000 competitors away. Their exodus will make room for him, his kindred and race, and create such a demand for labor, as he will reason it, to give him high wages. He goes naturally for the measure, and becomes an emancipationist. While the slave is with us, the foreigner will not crowd us, which will postpone to a long day the affliction of nations, an excess of population; the slaves away, the great tide of immigration will set in upon us, and precipitate upon our happy land this, the chief misery of most of the countries of Europe. Look at the myriads who are perpetually pouring into the northwestern states from the German hives—making large and exclusive settlements for themselves, which in a few years will number their thousands and tens of thousands, living in isolation; speaking a strange language, having alien manners, habits, opinions, and religious faiths, and a total ignorance of our political institutions; all handed down with German phlegm and inflexibility to their children through

This picture shows immigrants bound for the United States. Many Americans were afraid that unchecked immigration would cause race and religious conflicts.

generations. In less than fifty years, northern Illinois, parts of Ohio, and Michigan, Wisconsin, Iowa, and Minnesota will be literally possessed by them; they will number millions and millions, and they will be essentially a distinct people, a nation within a nation, a new Germany. We can't keep these people wholly out, and ought not if we could; but we are getting more than our share of them. I wish they would turn their direction to South America, quite as good a portion of the world as our share of the hemisphere. They could there aid in bringing up the slothful and degenerate Spanish race; here their deplorable office is to pull us down. . . . Let us withdraw from the newcomers the premium of political sovereignty. These strangers have neither the right nor the competency to govern the native-born people, nor ought they to be allowed the power to misgovern them. It is our right and our duty to govern ourselves, and them too when they come among us; and it is best for all parties that it should be so, and this difficult and important work can be better performed without their taking part in it, even when their intentions are good; but, misdirected and perverted by designing and wicked men, it is fatal infatuation to allow it. This truly foreign power nestled in the bosom of our country may, in its arch and crooked policy, occasionally act with one or another of the parties that spring up inherent in this republic. But it has its own paramount ends to circumvent; and when it seems to ally itself to any party, it is only a ruse; and the true motive is the belief that it helps on to the consummation of those ends. . . .

Mr. President, no well-informed and observant man can look abroad over this widespread and blessed country without feeling deep anxiety for the future. Some elements of discord and disunion are even now in fearful action. Spread out to such a vast extent, filling up almost in geometrical progression with communities and colonies from many lands, various as Europe in personal and national characteristics, in opinions, in manners and customs, in tongues and religious faiths, in the traditions of the past, and the objects and the hopes of the future, the United States can, no more than Europe, become one homogeneous mass—one peaceful, united, harmonizing, all self-adhering people. When the country shall begin to teem with people, these jarring elements being brought into proximity, their repellant and explosive properties will begin to act with greater intensity; and then, if not before, will come the war of geographical sections, the war of races, and the most relentless of all wars, of hostile religions. This mournful catastrophe will have been greatly hastened by our immense expansion and our proclamation to all mankind to become a part of us.

Unchecked Chinese Immigration

Edwin R. Meade

Edwin R. Meade, a Democratic congressman from
New York from 1875 until 1877, takes a hard-line approach to what he sees as the "evil" of Chinese immigration in the late nineteenth century. Though business and
industry leaders of the time utilized Chinese labor prof-
itably, some Americans, including Meade, felt that the
"coolies," a derogatory term for Chinese laborers, posed
innumerable problems for white people, including job
competition, lower wages, and corruption of American
democracy. Anti-Sino legislation received wide public
support, and, according to Meade, even the Chinese already in America opposed liberalizing anti-Asian immigration laws.

In the following 1877 address to the Social Science
Association of America, Meade explicates the threat
posed to American stability by immigrants from the
"Asiatic hive."

C hina is the most densely settled country on the globe,
and with its outlying and tributary provinces com-
prises something over 500 million population, or
about one-third of the world's mankind. It is largely over-
populated, especially with the labor element, and, considering the shortness of the time its ports have been open, its
people have proved themselves the most migratory of any nation. They are already to be found in nearly every country on

Edwin R. Meade, speech delivered to the Social Science Association of America
annual meeting, Saratoga, NY, September 7, 1877.

the earth and in this country have pitched a residence in every considerable town. Their passage to this country varies in expense per capita from $12 to $400.

They follow the great lines of travel, thus making their way to our Eastern Seaboard as fast as means and opportunities permit. New York City now contains about 2,000 coolies, while opium dens and a joss house already mark the eastward march of their peculiar civilization. In the Pacific states, Australia, Luzon, Java, Straits Settlements, Borneo, Peru, Cuba, and British Guiana, the coolie face and dress have become as familiar as those of the white laborer. From their Asiatic hive they still come pouring forth, and it is fair to presume will increase in volume as the advantages offered by the outside world in wages and liberal government become better known, accelerated, too, by the famines, internal wars, and pestilence which so frequently devastate their own country.

The term "coolie," however, does not imply a condition of servitude, as various public accounts, including the platforms of both political parties in 1876 would indicate. . . .

The coolie comes to our shores voluntarily. As a slave, or one held under conditions of servitude, he would be subject to ordinary methods of legislation, and public sentiment would scarcely be divided respecting him; but, as now presented, he becomes a question of desirability, and the proper course at issue to prevent his further introduction becomes a very serious problem.

Animal Machines

As suggested, he comes here as a laborer. He personifies the character in its absolutely menial aspect—what the operation of fifty centuries of paganism, poverty, and oppression have made him—a mere animal machine, performing the duties in his accepted sphere, punctually and patiently, but utterly incapable of any improvement; and in this aspect of the question the most serious phase of the problem is presented.

The qualities of coolie labor mentioned, and the fact that it can be secured in any desired amount and discharged without controversy, renders it especially attractive to capitalists and contractors. African slave labor presented to some extent the same features, but in a marked degree coolie labor is cheaper and therefore competitive with white labor. . . .

Recent disturbances in regard to labor show the importance of this aspect of the question and irresistibly awaken the conviction that cheap labor is not desirable in this country; and whatever folly there may be in the idea of establishing a minimum of wages by the government, it may properly withdraw encouragement from cheap labor even at the expense of dividends on diluted capital, as represented in watered stock. We require liberal wages to meet high tariffs, high taxes, and heavy charges of transportation. Coolie labor means to white labor starvation, almshouses, prisons filled, and, lastly, capital wasting itself. Liberal wages and white labor mean prosperity for all classes and progress in the ways of Christian civilization. All fancied advantages which have followed the introduction of coolies in this country disappear before the prospects to which their future in this country would invite us. . . .

An Unqualified Electorate

A republican or even liberal government of any form is to them quite incomprehensible. Government to their minds is a despotic power, in which they have no lot or part except unqualified obedience. If sufficiently intelligent, they point to the duration, the extent, and the achievements of the Celestial Empire and contrast them with our own country of a hundred years only of existence. Their superstitions, prejudices, and opinions have become as fixed as their habits of life, and their observations only disclose the apparent defects, contradictions, and inconsistencies in our government and religion, which to their minds is radical evidence of their general character. . . .

If he seems to conform to our ways, it is only to get a better foothold for moneymaking. He professes friendship, of which sentiment he has not the remotest conception. He is cruel and unrelenting, only waiting the opportunity in which he may safely strike the object of his spite, cupidity, or superstition. . . .

The people on the Pacific Coast describe the coolie as devoid of conscience. He has evidently never made sufficient use of one to cause it to be a prominent element of his character, or, at least, he manifests it after a different manner from ourselves. He has no respect for our form of oath; and no other form has been devised which reaches his mythical conscience or makes him tell the truth further than he regards it for his interest so to do. . . .

That we are bound to receive this alien influx is, I fancy, a piece of sentimentalism, which will not be accepted. Our social nature repels the idea, and our political system revolts at the reception of such a strange, unamalgamating, unassimilating, unnatural element. Of different planes, possessing widely divergent characteristics, we but invite the irrepressible conflict of races by recognizing for the time the equality of this Asiatic invasion. We boast that the Anglo-Saxon conquers or absorbs but never recognizes equality in other races; but we cannot overlook the fact that the Chinese nation has lasted from the dawn of centuries; that its government and people have witnessed the birth, decay, and dissolution of the greatest empires and republics that have existed; and that they now confront us upon the shores of the Pacific with a host which, by force of numbers alone, is able to convert this broad land into a Chinese colony, and the valley of the Mississippi a new battlefield of the races. . . .

The assertion that Chinese will not bring their families here is abundantly refuted in the exceptions which already exist, and also is an error the further statement that they do not desire citizenship. In conversation with their more intelligent people, they distinctly stated their desire to become citizens, which has doubtless been increased by observing the influence which their natural enemy, the "hoodlum," possesses, and as a protection from his indignities. The Chinese are, moreover, subjected to all the taxation of whites and, in instances, taxes discriminating against them. To be sure their taxable property, especially real estate, is comparatively small, but we must recognize the principle which extends the privilege of suffrage to all who bear taxation, unless we propose to erect a caste in our midst. Indeed the arguments are so strong in favor of citizenship, if we allow unrestricted immigration, that common justice, even if disguising the partisan seeking mere party ends, will succeed in making our naturalization laws, at least, as liberal toward the Chinaman as the wild African fresh from his native jungles.

Genetically Inferior

It is true that ethnologists declare that a brain capacity of less than eighty-five inches is unfit for free government, which is considerably above that of the coolie as it is below the Caucasian, but, whatever its merits, the statement will scarce stand in the way of either the demands of a justice recognized in the case of the Negro or where party advantages demand the concession. These coolies are, as mentioned, generally made up of males of voting age. Their number is already sufficient, of voters acting together, to now control the politics of the Pacific states, and there is good reason to believe that they would thus act, and under direction of their headmen.

The inference would seem, therefore, irresistible that the coolie, if permitted to immigrate here, must be received as an equal factor in our social policy and system, including the elective franchise, or else we must turn back the hands on the dial plate and reestablish a caste approaching servitude. The latter, I believe, utterly inadmissible, as, I believe, the former fraught with evils to our race and civilization, the like of which have not been chronicled in all the broad pages of the history of man.

An embarrassment in the way of a proper treatment of this subject is our generally declared policy in favor of unrestricted immigration and the right of self-expatriation. The error in this respect lies in classing this exceptional and peculiar people along with those of other countries and the white race; but, however much at variance with such a policy, we cannot afford to hesitate in the application of necessary measures to prevent this hurtful immigration. To accomplish this, without disturbing our valuable and growing commercial relations with the Chinese empire, requires careful consideration. For this purpose alone the treaty-making branch of government is preferable to Congress. Many of the alleged difficulties in the way disappear upon investigation.

For instance, we find that the influential Chinese in this

country favor either prohibition or a large restriction of coolie immigration, and such a course the Chinese merchants in San Francisco have, on several occasions, advised. This they are led to do by way of accommodating public sentiment, in which they concur, and because of the disadvantages to prosperous relations between the two countries if this irritating cause be not removed before it shall have been become firmly established. The Chinese national policy is also opposed to the emigration of its subjects. "To stay at home and mind their own business, and let other people do the same" has for centuries been the maxim of Chinese statesmen and sages, and the edicts against emigration have never been repealed, notwithstanding their repugnance to the provisions of their treaties with "the barbarians," as they are wont to style us. It is not unlikely, however, that a discrimination by us against their people, and without the assent of the Pekin government, would be received with disfavor and result in counteraction on the part of the Chinese. . . .

Whatever is done should be done without further delay; for delay will only fasten the evil of coolie population upon us. Chinese merchants, capitalists, and students, as well as those representing the Pekin government, deserve our kindest encouragement and protection. A Chinese embassy, soon to be permanently established here, and a Chinese consulship in San Francisco will tend to a better understanding of the character of that remarkable people and the resources of their country, while a professorship of Chinese literature, just established by one of our leading colleges, will explain the mysteries of its philosophy, science, and art; but the dignity of American labor and citizenship, and the welfare and renown of the white race, and an elevated and Christian civilization, alike, demand the exclusion of coolie immigrants.

Preserving the American Race

Henry Cabot Lodge

Harvard-educated Henry Cabot Lodge earned his doctorate in political science before ultimately joining the Harvard faculty and eventually running for Congress. Elected in 1893 to the Senate as a conservative Republican from Massachusetts, Lodge introduced a bill in 1896 which restricted immigration due to what Lodge saw as the incompatibility of non-Anglo-Saxons with American life. The particulars of his bill included, among other things, the establishment of literacy tests and an immigrant tax.

In his concluding argument for the bill, excerpted here, Lodge draws heavily on racial differences and the premise of Anglo-Saxon superiority.

I t now remains for me to discuss . . . the advisability of restricting immigration. . . . This is a subject of the greatest magnitude and the most far-reaching importance. It has two sides, the economic and the social. As to the former, but few words are necessary. There is no one thing which does so much to bring about a reduction of wages and to injure the American wage earner as the unlimited introduction of cheap foreign labor through unrestricted immigration. Statistics show that the change in the race character of our immigration has been accompanied by a corresponding decline in its quality. The number of skilled mechanics and of persons trained to some occupation or pursuit has fallen off, while the number of those without occupation or training, that is,

Henry Cabot Lodge, speech before the United States Congress, March 16, 1896.

who are totally unskilled, has risen in our recent immigration to enormous proportions. This low, unskilled labor is the most deadly enemy of the American wage earner, and does more than anything else toward lowering his wages and forcing down his standard of living.

An attempt was made, with the general assent of both political parties, to meet this crying evil some years ago by the passage of what are known as the contract-labor laws. That legislation was excellent in intention but has proved of but little value in practice. It has checked to a certain extent the introduction of cheap, low-class labor in large masses into the United States. It has made it a little more difficult for such labor to come here, but the labor of this class continues to come, even if not in the same way, and the total amount of it has not been materially reduced. Even if the contract-labor laws were enforced intelligently and thoroughly, there is no reason to suppose that they would have any adequate effect in checking the evil which they were designed to stop. It is perfectly clear, after the experience of several years, that the only relief which can come to the American wage earner from the competition of low-class immigrant labor must be by general laws restricting the total amount of immigration and framed in such a way as to affect most strongly those elements of the immigration which furnish the low, unskilled, and ignorant foreign labor.

It is not necessary to enter further into a discussion of the economic side of the general policy of restricting immigration. In this direction the argument is answerable.

Unfair Competition

If we have any regard for the welfare, the wages, or the standard of life of American workingmen, we should take immediate steps to restrict foreign immigration. There is no danger, at present at all events, to our workingmen from the coming of skilled mechanics or of trained and educated men with a settled occupation or pursuit, for immigrants of this class will never seek to lower the American standard of life and wages. On the contrary, they desire the same standard for themselves. But there is an appalling danger to the American wage earner from the flood of low, unskilled, ignorant, foreign labor which has poured into the country for some years past, and which not only takes lower wages but accepts a standard of life and living so low that the American workingman can not compete with it.

I now come to the aspect of this question which is graver and more serious than any other. The injury of unrestricted immigration to American wages and American standards of living is sufficiently plain and is bad enough, but the danger which this immigration threatens to the quality of our citizenship is far worse. That which it concerns us to know and that which is more vital to us as a people than all possible questions of tariff or currency is whether the quality of our citizenship is endangered by the present course and character of immigration to the United States. To determine this question intelligently we must look into the history of our race. . . .

A Question of Race

For practical purposes in considering a question of race and in dealing with the civilized peoples of western Europe and of America, there is no such thing as a race of original purity according to the divisions of ethnical science. In considering the practical problems of the present time, we can deal only with artificial races—that is, races like the English-speaking people, the French, or the Germans—who have been developed as races by the operation during a long period of time of climatic influences, wars, migrations, conquests, and industrial development. To the philologist and the ethnologist it is of great importance to determine the ethnical divisions of mankind in the earliest historic times. To the scientific modern historian, to the student of social phenomena, and to the statesman alike the early ethnic divisions are of little consequence, but the sharply marked race divisions which have been gradually developed by the conditions and events of the last thousand years are absolutely vital. . . .

The English-speaking race . . . has been made slowly during the centuries. Nothing has happened thus far to radically change it here. In the United States, after allowing for the variations produced by new climatic influences and changed conditions of life and of political institutions, it is still in the great essentials fundamentally the same race. The additions in this country until the present time have been from kindred people or from those with whom we have been long allied and who speak the same language. By those who look at this question superficially we hear it often said that the English-speaking people, especially in America, are a mixture of races. Analysis shows that the actual mixture of blood in the English-speaking race is very small, and that while the English-speaking people are derived through different channels, no doubt, there is among them nonetheless an overwhelming preponderance of the same race stock, that of the great Germanic tribes who reached from Norway to the Alps. They have been welded together by more than a thousand years of wars, conquests, migrations, and struggles, both at home and abroad, and in so doing they have attained a fixity and definiteness of national character unknown to any other people. . . .

A Moral Question

When we speak of a race, then, we do not mean its expressions in art or in language, or its achievements in knowledge. We mean the moral and intellectual characters, which in their association make the soul of a race and which represent the product of all its past, the inheritance of all its ancestors, and the motives of all its conduct. The men of each race possess an indestructible stock of ideas, traditions, sentiments, modes of thought, an unconscious inheritance from their ancestors, upon which argument has no effect. What makes a race are their mental and, above all, their moral characteristics, the slow growth and accumulation of centuries of toil and conflict. These are the qualities which determine their social efficiency as a people, which make one race rise and another fall, which we draw out of a dim past through many generations of ancestors, about which we cannot argue, but in which we blindly believe, and which guide us in our short-lived generation as they have guided the race itself across the centuries. . . .

Those qualities are moral far more than intellectual, and it is on the moral qualities of the English-speaking race that our history, our victories, and all our future rest. There is only one way in which you can lower those qualities or weaken those characteristics and that is by breeding them out. If a lower race mixes with a higher in sufficient numbers, history teaches us that the lower race will prevail. The lower race will absorb the higher, not the higher the lower, when the two strains approach equality in numbers. In other words, there is a limit to the capacity of any race for assimilating and elevating an inferior race, and when you begin to pour in unlimited numbers people of alien or lower races of less social efficiency and less moral force, you are running the most frightful risk that any people can run. The lowering of a great race means not only its own decline but that of human civilization. . . .

Danger on the Horizon

Mr. President, more precious even than forms of government are the mental and moral qualities which make what we call our race. While those stand unimpaired, all is safe. When those decline, all is imperiled. They are exposed to but a single danger and that is by changing the quality of our race and citizenship through the wholesale infusion of races whose traditions and inheritances, whose thoughts and whose beliefs are wholly alien to ours and with whom we have never assimilated or even been associated in the past. The danger has begun. It is small as yet, comparatively speaking, but it is large enough to warn us to act while there is yet time and while it can be done easily and efficiently. There lies the peril at the portals of our land; there is pressing in the tide of unrestricted immigration.

The time has certainly come, if not to stop at least to check, to sift, and to restrict those immigrants. In careless strength, with generous hand, we have kept our gates wide open to all the world. If we do not close them, we should at least place sentinels beside them to challenge those who would pass through. The gates which admit men to the United States and to citizenship in the great republic should no longer be left unguarded.

Shut the Door on Immigration

Ellison DuRant Smith

In the early twentieth century a large influx of Eastern European immigrants triggered overwhelming public support for laws that would restrict future immigration. During congressional debate over the bill that later became the Johnson-Reed Act of 1924 (aka the Immigration Act of 1924), the overwhelming majority of senators supported restrictive measures in one form or another.

In this speech Senator Ellison DuRant Smith, a South Carolina Democrat, invokes the unapologetic racist theories of Madison Grant in support of the 1924 act. Smith claims that Americans must "shut the door" on potential immigrants to the United States or risk overcrowding and the depletion of natural resources vital to the country's growth.

I
t seems to me . . . the time has arrived when we should shut the door. We have been called the melting pot of the world. We had an experience just a few years ago, during the great World War, when it looked as though we had allowed influences to enter our borders that were about to melt the pot in place of us being the melting pot.

I think that we have sufficient stock in America now for us to shut the door, Americanize what we have, and save the resources of America for the natural increase of our population. We all know that one of the most prolific causes of war is the desire for increased land ownership for the overflow of

Ellison DuRant Smith, speech before the United States Congress, April 9, 1924.

a congested population. We are increasing at such a rate that in the natural course of things in a comparatively few years the landed resources, the natural resources of the country, shall be taken up by the natural increase of our population. It seems to me the part of wisdom now that we have throughout the length and breadth of continental America a population which is beginning to encroach upon the reserve and virgin resources of the country to keep it in trust for the multiplying population of the country.

I do not believe that political reasons should enter into the discussion of this very vital question. It is of greater concern to us to maintain the institutions of America, to maintain the principles upon which this Government is founded, than to develop and exploit the underdeveloped resources of the country. There are some things that are dearer to us, fraught with more benefit to us, than the immediate development of the undeveloped resources of the country. I believe that our particular ideas, social, moral, religious, and political, have demonstrated, by virtue of the progress we have made and the character of people that we are, that we have the highest ideals of any member of the human family or any nation. We have demonstrated the fact that the human family, certainly the predominant breed in America, can govern themselves by a direct government of the people. If this Government shall fail, it shall fail by virtue of the terrible law of inherited tendency. Those who come from the nations which from time immemorial have been under the dictation of a master fall more easily by the law of inheritance and the inertia of habit into a condition of political servitude than the descendants of those who cleared the forests, conquered the savage, stood at arms and won their liberty from their mother country, England.

Madison Grant

I think we now have sufficient population in our country for us to shut the door and to breed up a pure, unadulterated American citizenship. I recognize that there is a dangerous lack of distinction between people of a certain nationality and the breed of the dog. Who is an American? Is he an immigrant from Italy? Is he an immigrant from Germany? If you were to go abroad and some one were to meet you and say, "I met a typical American," what would flash into your mind as a typical American, the typical representative of that new Nation? Would it be the son of an Italian immigrant, the son of a German immigrant, the son of any of the breeds from the Orient, the son of the denizens of Africa? We must not get our ethnological distinctions mixed up with our anthropological distinctions. It is the breed of the dog in which I am interested. I would like for the Members of the Senate to read that book just recently published by Madison Grant, *The Passing of a Great Race* (1918). Thank God we have in America perhaps the largest percentage of any country in the world of the pure, unadulterated Anglo-Saxon stock; certainly the greatest of any nation in the Nordic breed. It is for the preservation of that splendid stock that has characterized us that I would make this not an asylum for the oppressed of all countries, but a country to assimilate and perfect that splendid type of manhood that has made America the foremost Nation in her progress and in her power, and yet the youngest of all the nations. I myself believe that the preservation of her institutions depends upon us now taking counsel with our condition and our experience during the last World War.

Without offense, but with regard to the salvation of our own, let us shut the door and assimilate what we have, and let us breed pure American citizens and develop our own American resources. I am more in favor of that than I am of our quota proposition. Of course, it may not meet the approbation of the Senate that we shall shut the door—which I unqualifiedly and unreservedly believe to be our duty—and develop what we have, assimilate and digest what we have into pure Americans, with American aspirations, and thoroughly familiar with the love of American institutions, rather than the importation of any number of men from other countries. If we may not have that, then I am in favor of putting the quota down to the lowest possible point, with every selective element in it that may be.

The great desideratum [need] of modern times has been education, not alone book knowledge, but that education which enables men to think right, to think logically, to think truthfully, men equipped with power to appreciate the rapidly developing conditions that are all about us, that have converted the world in the last 50 years into a brand new world and made us masters of forces that are revolutionizing production. We want men not like dumb, driven cattle from those nations where the progressive thought of the times has scarcely made a beginning and where they see men as mere machines; we want men who have an appreciation of the responsibility brought about by the manifestation of the power of that individual. We have not that in this country to-day. We have men here to-day who are selfishly utilizing the enormous forces discovered by genius, and if we are not careful as statesmen, if we are not careful in our legislation, these very masters of the tremendous forces that have been made available to us will bring us under their domination and control by virtue of the power they have in multiplying their wealth.

We are struggling to-day against the organized forces of man's brain multiplied a million times by materialized thought in the form of steam and electricity as applied in the everyday affairs of man. We have enough in this country to engage the brain of every lover of his country in solving the problems of a democratic government in the midst of the imperial power that genius is discovering and placing in the hands of man. We have population enough to-day without throwing wide our doors and jeopardizing the interests of this country by pouring into it men who willingly become the slaves of those who employ them in manipulating these forces of nature, and they few reap the enormous benefits that accrue therefrom. . . .

We do not want to tangle the skein of America's progress by those who imperfectly understand the genius of our Government and the opportunities that lie about us. Let us keep what we have, protect what we have, make what we have the realization of the dream of those who wrote the Constitution.

I am more concerned about that than I am about whether a new railroad shall be built or whether there shall be diversified farming next year or whether a certain coal mine shall be mined. I would rather see American citizenship refined to the last degree in all that makes America what we hope it will be than to develop the resources of America at the expense of the citizenship of our country. The time has come when we should shut the door and keep what we have for what we hope our own people to be.

Immigration Quotas Are Necessary

Marion Moncure Duncan

On August 10, 1964, Marion Moncure Duncan, president general of the Daughters of the American Revolution (DAR), informed the House of Representatives Judiciary Committee that her organization vehemently opposed modification of the quotas established by the Immigration and Nationality Act of 1952. Duncan in her testimony expresses her organization's concern for immigrants, but she insists that the importance of this act can not be overestimated. According to Duncan, the DAR believes in retaining the quotas because of the negative effect certain immigrants have on America's economy and because of possible threats to national security such as infiltration by Communists.

M r. Chairman and members of the committee, thank you for your courtesy and indulgence in permitting me the opportunity to speak today. As president general, I officially represent the National Society, Daughters of the American Revolution, a nonpolitical organization dedicated to historic, educational, and patriotic objectives, whose membership runs approximately 185,000 in the 50 States, the District of Columbia, and some oversea units, comprising nearly 3,000 local chapter groups.

I speak in support of maintaining the existing provisions of the Immigration and Nationality Act of 1952, especially the national origins quota system, and against proposed lib-

Marion Moncure Duncan, statement before the United States House of Representatives Committee on the Judiciary, August 10, 1964.

eralizing amendments thereto, particularly, the deletion of the aforesaid national quota system and/or the establishment of a 5-year staggered accumulated immigration pool reserve.

Since you have already heard considerable testimony in past weeks, my remarks will be kept as brief as possible, stressing only the most pertinent points on which DAR membership has concern. In so doing, I speak not as a specialist or authority in a particular field. Rather, the focus is that of attempting to present to you and ask your consideration of the conscientious convictions of an organization keenly and, more importantly, actively interested in this subject almost since its own inception nearly three-quarters of a century ago. Such interest actually dates back prior to the time any immigration statutes were of record. To substantiate this statement, lest there be any misconception such as was remarked to me in ignorance a year ago that "the DAR is against immigrants," with pride I point out as follows:

It was in 1913 the first—and for a number of years the only—naturalization school in this country was founded, operated, and financed by the DAR here in Washington, D.C., and continued so until the school was later incorporated— and still operates—in the District of Columbia school system.

Another tangible and definite example of this organization's interest in immigrants coming to America seeking citizenship has been the consistent and continuous printing over the years, since 1920 (oftimes in many languages) of the "DAR Manual for Citizenship." I have provided a copy for you gentlemen. In years past this has been sent abroad through an international committee to interest folks in coming to America.

Over 9 million copies of this volume have been donated free in an effort to aid and abet an adequate understanding and full appreciation of good citizenship among immigrants. Aside from the quantity supplied, many heartwarming letters attest the value and benefit of this endeavor.

DAR chapters and individuals regularly, year in and year out, sponsor programs and/or participate in connection with naturalization courts.

Further, there is an intangible factor having bearing on the matter at hand. It is the "personal followthrough" which has ever been an integral part of DAR interest in and service to worthy would-be Americans. Sometimes this means a dinner in the home, or a dentist or doctor referral for a sick family member. It can also culminate in a presentation ceremony where a prized DAR Americanism Award is given to a naturalized American in recognition of outstanding service to his new homeland. . . .

The DAR Is Concerned About Immigrants

Gentlemen, the purpose in reciting the foregoing points was twofold: First, to establish the fact that the National Society, Daughters of the American Revolution, has been and continues to be interested in this minority group of our population and that interest is based upon firsthand knowledge, personal and direct; further, and secondly, the effort is to assure you that in appearing here today . . . the DAR is not taking a stand against immigration per se. Any inference in that direction is in error and completely false. DAR, as a national organization, is among the foremost "to extend a helping hand" to immigrants admitted on an intelligent, orderly, equitable basis such as is allowed under the current Immigration and Nationality Act of 1952. If, from time to time, there be need for change or adjustment, it should be provided through logical, deliberate amendment, still retaining the national origins quota system and other vitally basic, protective features of the law. These constitute a first line of defense in perpetuating and maintaining our institutions of freedom and the American way of life. To discard them would endanger both.

From [the] point that immigration is definitely a matter of national welfare and security, it is imperative that a logical and rational method of governing and administering same be maintained. The [1952] Walter-McCarran Act has done and will continue equitably to accomplish just this. It denies no nation a quota, but it does provide a reasonable, orderly, mathematical formula (based, of course, upon the 1920 census figures) which is devoid of the political pressures which could inevitably be expected to beset any commission authorized to reapportion unused quotas as proposed in the legislation before you.

Historical Background and Importance of the 1952 Act

By way of background: What prompted passage of the Immigration-Nationality Act of 1952? It will be recalled that this was the product of a tedious, comprehensive study of nearly 5 years' duration, covering some 200 laws on selective immigration, special orders and exclusions, and spanned the period from passage of the first quota law by Congress in 1924. This law codified and coordinated all existing immigration, nationality, and deportation laws.

Despite repeated efforts to weaken, circumvent and bypass this protective legislation, its soundness has been demonstrated over the period it has been in operation.

It embodies the following important features—all in the best interest of our constitutional republic:

(a) Recognizing the cultural identity and historic population basis of this Nation, it officially preserved the national origin quota system as the basis for immigration, wisely giving preference to those nations whose composite culture—Anglo-Saxon from northern and western European countries—has been responsible for and actually produced the American heritage as we know it today.

(b) It abolished certain discriminatory provisions in our immigration laws—those against sexes and persons of Asiatic origin.

(c) "Quality versus quantity" preference for skilled aliens was provided, as well as broadened classifications for non-quota immigrants. No nation or race is listed ineligible for immigration and naturalization, although the acknowledged purpose is to preserve this country's culture, free institutions, free enterprise economy and racial complex, yes, and likely even language. Ready assimilability of the majority of immigrants is a prime factor.

(d) It provides the U.S. Immigration Department with needed authority to cope with subversive aliens by strengthening security provisions.

Perhaps the sentiment and deep concern of the DAR relative to the matter of immigration and its appeal for retention of the present law is best expressed by excerpting salient points from recent resolutions on the subject:

(1) For building unity and cohesiveness among American citizens, whose social, economic and spiritual mind has been and is under increasing pressures and conflicts, wise and comprehensive steps must be taken.

(2) For the protection and interest of all citizens from foreign elements imbued with ideologies wholly at variance with our republican form of government should be excluded.

On basis of FBI [Federal Bureau of Investigation] analysis statistics and information available through investigation by the House Un-American Activities Committee, loopholes through which thousands of criminal aliens may enter this country constitute a continuing threat for the safety of American institutions.

(3) Since it is a recognized fact that free migration allowing unhampered movement of agents is necessary for triumph of either a world socialist state or international communism as a world conspiracy, this would explain the motivation on the part of enemies of this country for concentrated effort to undermine the existing immigration law.

(4) Admittedly, major problems confronting the Nation and threatening its national economy are unemployment, housing, education, security, population explosion, and other domestic problems such as juvenile delinquency, crime, and racial tensions. This is borne out by numerous statistics and the current Federal war on poverty effort. In view of this, revisions as per proposed new quotas to greatly increase the number of immigrants would be a threat to the security and well-being of this Nation, especially in face of the cold war inasmuch as it would be impossible to obtain adequate security checks on immigrants from satellite Communist-controlled countries.

In summation: A comparative study would indicate increased aggravation of existing problems and unfavorable repercussions on all facets of our economy such as employment, housing, education, welfare, health, and national security, offering additional threat to the American heritage—cultural, social, and ethnic traditions. . . .

While DAR would be the first to admit the importance of immigrants to America, its membership ties linking directly with the first waves of immigrants to these shores, it would seem well, however, to point out a "then and now" difference factor currently exists attributable to time and circumstance—no uncomplimentary inference therein. A common desire shared by immigrants of all time to America has been the seeking of freedom or the escape from tyranny. But in the early days, say the first 150 years, it is noteworthy that those who came shared common Anglo-Saxon bonds and arrived with the full knowledge and intent of founders or pioneers who knew there was a wilderness to conquer and a nation to build. Their coming indicated a willingness to make a contribution and assume such a role. In the intervening years, many fine, high-caliber immigrants, and I know some at personal sacrifice, following ideals in which they believed, have likewise come to America imbued with a constructive desire to produce and add to the glory of their new homeland. They, however, have come to a nation already established with cultural patterns set and traditions already rooted.

Further, in recent years, en masse refugee movements, though responding to the very same ideal which is America, have been motivated primarily by escape. This has had a tendency possibly to dim individual purpose and dedication and possibly project beyond other considerations, the available benefits to be secured as an American citizen.

Abandonment of the national origins system would drastically alter the source of our immigration. Any change would not take into consideration that those whose background and heritage most closely resemble our own are most readily assimilable. . . .

Not a Right but a Privilege

Attention is called to the fact that immigration is not an alien's right; it is a privilege. With privilege comes its handmaiden responsibility. Before tampering with the present immigration law, much less destroying its basic principles, due regard must also be given to our own unemployment situation. No less an authority than the late President John F. Kennedy, who was for this bill, stated on March 3, 1963, that we had 5 million unemployed and 2 million people displaced each year by advancing technology and automation.

Irrespective of recent and recurring reports on unemployment showing temporary increases or decreases, the fact is, it remains a matter of economic concern. Latest figures available as of June 1964 indicate 4.7 million or 5.3 percent.

In view of this, it would seem highly incongruent if not outright incredible to find ourselves in a situation, on the one hand, waging war on poverty and unemployment at home, while on the other hand, simultaneously and indiscriminately letting down immigration bars to those abroad. Not only employment alone but mental health and retardation problems could greatly increase. Another source of concern to the heavy laden taxpayer to whom already the national debt figure is astronomical.

It is asserted that our economy will get three consumers for every worker admitted and that our economy generates jobs at a rate better than one for every three consumers. Why, then, are we presently plagued with unemployment? And how is it possible to guarantee that these new immigrants will "fill jobs that are going begging because there are not enough skilled workers in our economy who have the needed skills?" Are there enough such jobs going begging to justify destroying an immigration law which has been described as our first line of defense?

Rightly, it would seem U.S. citizens should have first claim on jobs and housing in this country. With manpower available and the recent emphasis on expanded educational facilities, why is not definite concentrated effort made to provide and accelerate vocational and special skill training for the many who either through disinclination, native inability or otherwise are not qualified potentials for schooling in the field of science, medicine, law, or other such professions?

Without the quota system, it is doubtful whether or not America could indefinitely maintain its traditional heritage: Economic, cultural, social, ethnic, or even language.

Free institutions as we have known them would stand to undergo radical change if the proposal to permit reapportionment of unused quotas is also adopted. It is felt reassignment of unused quotas would be as damaging to the basic principles of the Immigration and Nationality Act as repeal of the national origins system itself. The proviso that the President reserve a portion of the pool for allocation to qualified immigrants further extends the power of the executive branch of the Government.

Communist Infiltration

No less important is the fact that it is almost impossible to adequately screen persons coming from satellite countries.

It may well be embarrassing to proponents of liberalizing amendments to find that some of the most active opposition against the Walter-McCarran Act is provided by the Communists. According to the House Committee on Un-American Activities, the Communist Party has created, and now controls, in 15 key States, 180 "front" organizations dedicated exclusively to the purpose of creating grassroots pressure in the Congress to destroy the act—which is what most of the proposed amendments would do.

In this connection, I am reminded of the expressive words of the late beloved poet, Robert Frost, who, in "A Poet's Reflections on America and the World," put it this way: "Sizing up America: You ask me if America is still a great country. Well, it's easy to see that, if we don't know how great America is, Russia does."

The National Society, Daughters of the American Revolution, which initially supported the Walter-McCarran bill when it was introduced and has continuously done so since, wishes again to officially reaffirm its support of the existing law, firmly believing that the present Immigration and Nationality Act of 1952 not only safeguards our constitutional Republic and perpetuates our American heritage, but by maintaining its established standards, that it actually protects the naturalized American on a par with the native born, and as well offers encouragement to desirable immigrants to become future American citizens. Any breakdown in this system would be an open invitation to Communist infiltration. Likewise, a poor law, newly enacted, and improperly administered, could provide the same opportunity to the detriment, if not the actual downfall, of our country.

The well-intentioned, humanitarian plea that America's

unrestricted assumption of the overpopulous, troubled, ailing people of the world within our own borders is unrealistic, impractical, and if done in excess could spell economic bankruptcy for our people from point of both employment and overladen taxes to say nothing of a collapse of morale and spiritual values if nonassimilable aliens of dissimilar ethnic background and culture by wholesale and indiscriminate transporting en masse overturn the balance of our national character.

In connection with the liberalization proposals, it would seem timely to refer to the words of Senator [Patrick] McCarran, who, when he presented the bill, warned:

> If the enemies of this legislation succeed in riddling it to pieces, or in amending it beyond recognition, they will have contributed more to promote this Nation's downfall than any other group since we achieved our independence as a nation.

Somewhat the same sentiment was expressed by Abraham Lincoln, who admonished:

> You cannot strengthen the weak by weakening the strong; and you cannot help men permanently by doing for them what they could and should do for themselves.

Many inspiring words have been written of America. I would conclude with those of the late historian, James Truslow Adams:

> America's greatest contribution to the world has been that of the American dream, the dream of a land where life shall be richer, fuller, and better, with opportunity for every person according to his ability and achievement.

The question is: Can it continue so if, through reckless abandon, the United States becomes mired, causing the country to lose its image as the land of opportunity, the home of the free? Ours is the responsibility to maintain and preserve it for the future.

A Selective Immigration Policy Will Ensure Social and Cultural Unity

Pat Buchanan

Political commentator Pat Buchanan worked on the White House staff of presidents Richard Nixon and Ronald Reagan and eventually ran for president himself in 1992. His campaign platform focused largely on the issue of immigration, specifically his plan to reduce entry visas to 300,000 per year.

In this speech from January 2000 Buchanan cites research that illustrates the negative economic impact of immigration and advocates an overhaul of U.S. immigration policy. He proposes both a point system to determine the worthiness of a potential immigrant and an increase in funding to combat illegal immigration, especially along the U.S.-Mexican border.

Let me begin with a story: In 1979, Deng Xiaoping arrived here on an official visit. China was emerging from the Cultural Revolution, and poised to embark on the capitalist road. When President [Jimmy] Carter sat down with Mr. Deng, he told him he was concerned over the right of the Chinese people to emigrate. The Jackson-Vanik amendment, Mr. Carter said, prohibited granting most fa-

---

Pat Buchanan, speech delivered at Richard Nixon Library, Yorba Linda, CA, January 18, 2000. Copyright © 2000 by Pat Buchanan. Reproduced by permission.

vored nation trade status to regimes that did not allow their people to emigrate.

"Well, Mr. President," Deng cheerfully replied, "Just how many Chinese do you want? Ten million. Twenty million. Thirty million?" Deng's answer stopped Carter cold. In a few words, the Chinese leader had driven home a point Mr. Carter seemed not to have grasped: Hundreds of millions of people would emigrate to America in a eyelash, far more than we could take in, far more than our existing population of 270 million, if we threw open our borders. And though the U.S. takes in more people than any other nation, it still restricts immigration to about one million a year, with three or four hundred thousand managing to enter every year illegally.

There is more to be gleaned from this encounter. Mr. Carter's response was a patriotic, or, if you will, a nationalistic response. Many might even label it xenophobic. The President did not ask whether bringing in 10 million Chinese would be good for them. He had suddenly grasped that the real issue was how many would be good for America? Mr. Carter could have asked another question: Which Chinese immigrants would be best for America? It would make a world of difference whether China sent over 10 million college graduates or 10 million illiterate peasants, would it not?

Since the Carter-Deng meeting, America has taken in 20 million immigrants, many from China and Asia, many more from Mexico, Central America and the Caribbean, and a few from Europe. Social scientists now know a great deal about the impact of this immigration.

Many Immigrants Love America

Like all of you, I am awed by the achievements of many recent immigrants. Their contributions to Silicon Valley [where much of the computer industry is based] are extraordinary. The over-representation of Asian-born kids in advanced high school math and science classes is awesome, and, to the extent that it is achieved by a superior work ethic, these kids are setting an example for all of us. The contributions that immigrants make in small businesses and hard work in tough jobs that don't pay well merits our admiration and deepest respect. And, many new immigrants show a visible love of this country and an appreciation of freedom that makes you proud to be an American.

Northern Virginia, where I live, has experienced a huge and sudden surge in immigration. It has become a better place, in some ways, but nearly unrecognizable in others, and no doubt worse in some realms, a complicated picture over all. But it is clear to anyone living in a state like California or Virginia that the great immigration wave, set in motion by the Immigration Act of 1965, has put an indelible mark upon America.

We are no longer a biracial society; we are now a multiracial society. We no longer struggle simply to end the divisions and close the gaps between black and white Americans; we now grapple, often awkwardly, with an unprecedented ethnic diversity. We also see the troubling signs of a national turning away from the idea that we are one people, and the emergence of a radically different idea, that we are separate ethnic nations within a nation. . . .

Current Policy Is Skewed

We have a National Academy of Sciences report on the economic consequences of immigration, a Rand study, and work by Harvard's George Borjas and other scholars. All agree that new immigration to the United States is heavily skewed to admitting the less skilled. Unlike other industrialized democracies, the U.S. allots the vast majority of its visas on the basis of whether new immigrants are related to recent immigrants, rather than whether they have the skills or education America needs. This is why it is so difficult for Western and Eastern Europeans to come here, while almost entire villages from El Salvador have come in.

Major consequences flow from having an immigration stream that ignores education or skills. Immigrants are now more likely than native-born Americans to lack a high school education. More than a quarter of our immigrant population receives some kind of welfare, compared to 15 percent of native-born. Before the 1965 bill, immigrants were less likely to receive welfare. In states with many immigrants, the fiscal impact is dramatic. The National Academy of Sciences contends that immigration has raised the annual taxes of each native household in California by $1,200 a year. But the real burden is felt by native-born workers, for whom mass immigration means stagnant or falling wages, especially for America's least skilled.

There are countervailing advantages. Businesses can hire new immigrants at lower pay; and consumers gain because reduced labor costs produce cheaper goods and services. But, generally speaking, the gains from high immigration go to those who use the services provided by new immigrants.

If you are likely to employ a gardener or housekeeper, you may be financially better off. If you work as a gardener or housekeeper, or at a factory job in which unskilled immigrants are rapidly joining the labor force, you lose. The last twenty years of immigration have thus brought about a redistribution of wealth in America, from less-skilled workers and toward employers. Mr. Borjas estimates that one half of the relative fall in the wages of high school graduates since the 1980s can be traced directly to mass immigration.

At some point, this kind of wealth redistribution, from the less well off to the affluent, becomes malignant. In the 1950s and '60s, Americans with low reading and math scores could aspire to and achieve the American Dream of a middle class lifestyle. That is less realistic today. Americans today who do poorly in high school are increasingly condemned to a low-wage existence; and mass immigration is a major reason why.

There is another drawback to mass immigration: a delay in the assimilation of immigrants that can deepen our racial and ethnic divisions. . . .

Concerns of this sort are even older than the Republic itself. In 1751, Ben Franklin asked: "Why should Pennsylvania, founded by the English, become a Colony of Aliens, who will shortly be so numerous as to Germanize us instead of our Anglifying them?" Franklin would never find out if his fears were justified. German immigration was halted by the Seven Years War; then slowed by the Great Lull in immigration that followed the American Revolution. A century and a half later, during what is called the Great Wave, the same worries were in the air.

In 1915 Theodore Roosevelt told the Knights of Columbus: "There is no room in this country for hyphenated Americanism. . . . The one absolutely certain way of bringing this nation to ruin, of preventing all possibility of its continuing to be a nation at all, would be to permit it to become a tangle of squabbling nationalities." Congress soon responded by enacting an immigration law that brought about a virtual forty-year pause to digest, assimilate, and Americanize the diverse immigrant wave that had rolled in between 1890 and 1920.

Today, once again, it is impossible not to notice the conflict generated by a new "hyphenated Americanism." In Los Angeles, two years ago, there was an anguishing afternoon in the Coliseum where the U.S. soccer team was playing Mexico. The Mexican-American crowd showered the U.S. team with water bombs, beer bottles and trash. The Star Spangled Banner was hooted and jeered. A small contingent of fans of the American team had garbage hurled at them. The American players later said that they were better received in Mexico City than in their own country.

Last summer, El Cenizo, a small town in south Texas, adopted Spanish as its official language. All town documents are now to be written, and all town business conducted, in Spanish. Any official who cooperates with U.S. immigration authorities was warned he or she would be fired. To this day, Governor Bush is reluctant to speak out on this de facto secession of a tiny Texas town to Mexico.

Voting in referendums that play a growing part in the politics of California is now breaking down sharply on ethnic lines. Hispanic voters opposed Proposition 187 to cut off welfare to illegal aliens, and they rallied against it under Mexican flags. They voted heavily in favor of quotas and ethnic preferences in the 1996 California Civil Rights Initiative, and, again, to keep bilingual education in 1998. These votes suggest that in the California of the future, when Mexican-American voting power catches up with Mexican-American population, any bid to end racial quotas by referendum will fail. A majority of the state's most populous immigrant group now appears to favor set-asides and separate language programs, rather than to be assimilated into the American mainstream. The list of troubling signs can be extended. . . .

I don't want to overstate the negatives. But in too many cases the American Melting Pot has been reduced to a simmer. At present rates, mass immigration reinforces ethnic subcultures, reduces the incentives of newcomers to learn English; and extends the life of linguistic ghettos that might otherwise be melded into the great American mainstream. If we want to assimilate new immigrants—and we have no choice if we are to remain one nation—we must slow down the pace of immigration.

A Threat to Social Progress

Whatever its shortcomings, the United States has done far better at alleviating poverty than most countries. But an America that begins to think of itself as made up of disparate peoples will find social progress far more difficult. It is far easier to look the other way when the person who needs help does not speak the same language, or share a common culture or common history.

Americans who feel it natural and right that their taxes support the generation that fought World War II—will they feel the same way about those from Fukien Province or Zanzibar? If America continues on its present course, it could rapidly become a country with no common language, no common culture, no common memory and no common identity. And that country will find itself very short of the social cohesion that makes compassion possible.

None of us are true universalists: we feel responsibility for others because we share with them common bonds— common history and a common fate. When these are gone, this country will be a far harsher place.

That is why I am proposing immigration reform to make it possible to fully assimilate the 30 million immigrants who have arrived in the last thirty years. As President, I will ask Congress to reduce new entry visas to 300,000 a year, which is enough to admit immediate family members of new citizens, with plenty of room for many thousands with the special talents or skills our society needs. If after several years, it becomes plain that the United States needs more immigrants because of labor shortages, it should implement a point system similar to that of Canada and Australia, and allocate visas on a scale which takes into account education, knowledge of English, job skills, age, and relatives in the United States.

I will also make the control of illegal immigration a national priority. Recent reports of thousands of illegals streaming across the border into Arizona, and the sinister and cruel methods used to smuggle people by ship into the United States, demand that we regain control of our borders. For a country that cannot control its borders isn't fully sovereign; indeed, it is not even a country anymore.

Without these reforms, America will begin a rapid drift into uncharted waters. We shall become a country with a dying culture and deepening divisions along the lines of race, class, income and language. We shall lose for our children and for the children of the 30 million who have come here since 1970 the last best hope of earth. We will betray them all—by denying them the great and good country we were privileged to grow in. We just can't do that. With immigration at the reduced rate I recommend, America will still be a nation of immigrants. We will still have the benefit of a large, steady stream of people from all over the world whose life dream is to be like us—Americans. But, with this reform, America will become again a country engaged in the mighty work of assimilation, of shaping new Americans, a proud land where newcomers give up their hyphens, the great American melting pot does its work again, and scores of thousands of immigrant families annually ascend from poverty into the bosom of Middle America to live the American dream.

GREAT
SPEECHES
IN
HISTORY

Perspectives on Assimilation

Assimilation and the American Zionist

Richard Gottheil

At the end of the nineteenth century a massive Jewish population fled from anti-Semitic persecution found in Eastern Europe, and many tried to immigrate to America. Immigration restrictions in the United States delayed or denied entrance to thousands of these refugees, leaving them no place to go. According to some historians, the American Zionist movement developed out of the restrictive U.S. policies. The Zionists argued that an unreceptive America should then support the creation of a Jewish homeland in Israel, the region the Jews referred to as Zion.

In his closing remarks of an 1898 speech delivered in New York City, Richard Gottheil considers the meaning of the word "assimilation" and its particular relevance to Jews in America. Gottheil, a Columbia University professor of Semitic languages who campaigned vigorously for the American Federation of Zionists, concludes that the assimilation of Jews is not always possible because of rampant anti-Semitic feelings among host populations. Those Jews who are finding it possible to assimilate, however, should support the establishment of Zion because it will mean decreased Jewish immigration to America that will, in turn, abate anti-Semitic antagonism in the States.

I know that there are a great many of our people who look for a final solution of the Jewish question in what they call "assimilation." The more the Jews assimilate

Richard Gottheil, speech delivered in New York City, November 1, 1898.

themselves to their surroundings, they think, the more completely will the causes for anti-Jewish feeling cease to exist. But have you ever for a moment stopped to consider what assimilation means? It has very pertinently been pointed out that the use of the word is borrowed from the dictionary of physiology. But in physiology it is not the food which assimilates itself into the body. It is the body which assimilates the food. The Jew may wish to be assimilated; he may do all he will towards this end. But if the great mass in which he lives does not wish to assimilate him—what then? If demands are made upon the Jew which practically mean extermination, which practically mean his total effacement from among the nations of the globe and from among the religious forces of the world,—what answer will you give? And the demands made are practically of that nature.

The Barriers to Assimilation

I can imagine it possible for a people who are possessed of an active and aggressive charity which it expresses, not only in words, but also in deeds, to contain and live at peace with men of the most varied habits. But, unfortunately, such people do not exist; nations are swayed by feelings which are dictated solely by their own self-interests; and the Zionists in meeting this state of things, are the most practical as well as the most ideal of the Jews.

It is quite useless to tell the English workingman that his Jewish fellow-laborer from Russia has actually increased the riches of the United Kingdom; that he has created quite a new industry,—that of making ladies' cloaks, for which formerly England sent £2,000,000 to the continent every year. He sees in him some one who is different to himself, and unfortunately successful, though different. And until that difference entirely ceases, whether of habit, of way, or of religious observance, he will look upon him and treat him as an enemy.

For the Jew has this especial disadvantage. There is no place where that which is distinctively Jewish in his manner or in his way of life is à la mode. We may well laugh at the Irishman's brogue; but in Ireland, he knows, his brogue is at home. We may poke fun at the Frenchman as he shrugs his

shoulders and speaks with every member of his body. The
Frenchman feels that in France it is the proper thing so to do.
Even the Turk will wear his fez, and feel little the worse for
the occasional jibes with which the street boy may greet it.
But this consciousness, this ennobling consciousness, is all
denied the Jew. What he does is nowhere *à la mode*; no, not
even his features; and if he can disguise these by parting his
hair in the middle or cutting his beard to a point, he feels he
is on the road towards assimilation. He is even ready to use
the term "Jewish" for what he considers uncouth and low.

The Importance of a Homeland

For such as these amongst us, Zionism also has its message. It
wishes to give back to the Jew that nobleness of spirit, that
confidence in himself, that belief in his own powers which
only perfect freedom can give. With a home of his own, he
will no longer feel himself a pariah among the nations, he will
nowhere hide his own peculiarities,—peculiarities to which he
has a right as much as any one,—but will see that those peculiarities carry with them a message which will force for
them the admiration of the world. He will feel that he belongs
somewhere and not everywhere. He will try to be something
and not everything. The great word which Zionism preaches
is conciliation of conflicting aims, of conflicting lines of action; conciliation of Jew to Jew. It means conciliation of the
non-Jewish world to the Jew as well. It wishes to heal old
wounds; and by frankly confessing differences which do exist,
however much we try to explain them away, to work out its
own salvation upon its own ground, and from these to send
forth its spiritual message to a conciliated world.

Reaction of American Jews

But, you will ask, if Zionism is able to find a permanent
home in Palestine for those Jews who are forced to go there
as well as those who wish to go, what is to become of us who
have entered, to such a degree, into the life around us, and
who feel able to continue as we have begun? What is to be
our relation to the new Jewish polity? I can only answer: Ex-

actly the same as is the relation of people of other nationalities all the world over to their parent home. What becomes of the Englishman in every corner of the globe? What becomes of the German? Does the fact that the great mass of their people live in their own land prevent them from doing their whole duty towards the land in which they happen to live? Is the German-American considered less of an American because he cultivates the German language and is interested in the fate of his fellow-Germans at home? Is the Irish-American less of an American because he gathers money to help his struggling brethren in the Green Isle? Or are the Scandinavian-Americans less worthy of the title Americans, because they consider precious the bonds which bind them to the land of their birth, as well as those which bind them to the land of their adoption?

Nay! it would seem to me that just those who are so afraid that our action will be misinterpreted should be among the greatest helpers in the Zionist cause. For those who feel no racial and national communion with the life from which they have sprung should greet with joy the turning of Jewish immigration to some place other than the land in which they dwell. They must feel, for example, that a continual influx of Jews who are not Americans is a continual menace to the more or less complete absorption for which they are striving. . . .

We [the Zionists] believe that the Jews are something more than a purely religious body; that they are not only a race, but also a nation; though a nation without as yet two important requisites—a common home and a common language.

Americanism and the Foreign Born

Woodrow Wilson

Woodrow Wilson was president of the United States from 1913 to 1921. He witnessed a large influx of immigrants into the nation in the years just prior to America's involvement in World War I. As national and ethnic rivalries tore apart Europe, Wilson argued that immigrants to the United States must dedicate themselves to becoming Americans through assimilation and education. In the following 1915 address given at a swearing in of new U.S. citizens, Wilson says that the audience must now think of themselves as Americans rather than members of a particular ethnic group. Only by leaving their old ethnic allegiances behind them can new immigrants share in the ideals of liberty, justice, and opportunity that make the nation strong and unified.

I t warms my heart that you should give me such a reception, but it is not of myself that I wish to think to-night, but of those who have just become citizens of the United States. This is the only country in the world which experiences this constant and repeated rebirth. Other countries depend upon the multiplication of their own native people. This country is constantly drinking strength out of new sources by the voluntary association with it of great bodies of strong men and forward-looking women. And so by the gift of the free will of independent people it is constantly being renewed from generation to generation by the same

Woodrow Wilson, speech delivered to a swearing in of citizens, Philadelphia, PA, May 10, 1915.

process by which it was originally created. It is as if humanity had determined to see to it that this great nation, founded for the benefit of humanity, should not lack for the allegiance of the people of the world.

You have just taken an oath of allegiance to the United States. Of allegiance to whom? Of allegiance to no one, unless it be God. Certainly not of allegiance to those who temporarily represent this great Government. You have taken an oath of allegiance to a great ideal, to a great body of principles, to a great hope of the human race. You have said, "We are going to America," not only to earn a living, not only to seek the things which it was more difficult to obtain where you were born, but to help forward the great enterprises of the human spirit—to let man know that everywhere in the world there are men who will cross strange oceans and go where a speech is spoken which is alien to them, knowing that, whatever the speech, there is but one longing and utterance of the human heart, and that is for liberty and justice.

Think First of America

And while you bring all countries with you, you come with a purpose of leaving all other countries behind you—bringing what is best of their spirit, but not looking over your shoulders and seeking to perpetuate what you intended to leave in them. I certainly would not be one even to suggest that a man ceases to love the home of his birth and the nation of his origin—these things are very sacred and ought not to be put out of our hearts—but it is one thing to love the place where you were born and it is another thing to dedicate yourself to the place to which you go. You cannot dedicate yourself to America unless you become in every respect and with every purpose of your will thorough Americans. You cannot become thorough Americans if you think of yourselves in groups. America does not consist of groups. A man who thinks of himself as belonging to a particular national group in America, has not yet become an American, and the man who goes among you to trade upon your nationality is no worthy son to live under the Stars and Stripes. My urgent advice to you would be not only always to think first of America, but always, also, to think first of humanity. You do not love humanity if you seek to divide humanity into jealous camps. Humanity can be welded together only by love, by sympathy, by justice, not by jealousy and hatred. I am sorry for the man who seeks to make personal capital out of the passions of his fellow men. He has lost the touch and ideal of America, for America was created to unite mankind by those passions which lift and not by the passions which separate and debase.

To Be Rid of Divisions

We came to America, either ourselves or in the persons of our ancestors, to better the ideals of men, to make them see finer things than they had seen before, to get rid of things that divide, and to make sure of the things that unite. It was but an historical accident no doubt that this great country was called the "United States," and yet I am very thankful that it has the word "united" in its title; and the man who seeks to divide man from man, group from group, interest from interest, in the United States is striking at its very heart.

It is a very interesting circumstance to me, in thinking of those of you who have just sworn allegiance to this great Government, that you were drawn across the ocean by some beckoning finger of hope, by some belief, by some vision of a new kind of justice, by some expectation of a better kind of life.

No doubt you have been disappointed in some of us; some of us are very disappointing. No doubt you have found that justice in the United States goes only with a pure heart and a right purpose, as it does everywhere else in the world. No doubt what you found here didn't seem touched for you, after all, with the complete beauty of the ideal which you had conceived beforehand.

But remember this, if we had grown at all poor in the ideal, you brought some of it with you. A man does not go out to seek the thing that is not in him. A man does not hope for the thing that he does not believe in; and if some of us have forgotten what America believed in, you, at any rate, imported in your own hearts a renewal of the belief. That is the reason that I, for one, make you welcome.

If I have in any degree forgotten what America was intended for, I will thank God if you will remind me.

The Example of America

I was born in America. You dreamed dreams of what America was to be, and I hope you brought the dreams with you. No man that does not see visions will ever realize any high hope or undertake any high enterprise.

Just because you brought dreams with you, America is more likely to realize the dreams such as you brought. You are enriching us if you came expecting us to be better than we are.

See, my friends, what that means. It means that America must have a consciousness different from the consciousness of every other nation in the world. I am not saying this with even the slightest thought of criticism of other nations. You know how it is with a family. A family gets centered on itself if it is not careful and is less interested in the neighbors than it is in its own members. So a nation that is not constantly renewed out of new sources is apt to have the narrowness and prejudice of a family. Whereas, America must have this consciousness, that on all sides it touches elbows and touches hearts with all the nations of mankind.

The example of America must be a special example. The example of America must be the example not merely of peace because it will not fight, but of peace because peace is the healing and elevating influence of the world and strife is not.

There is such a thing as a man being too proud to fight. There is such a thing as a nation being so right that it does not need to convince others by force that it is right.

So, if you come into this great nation as you have come, voluntarily seeking something that we have to give, all that we have to give is this: We cannot exempt you from work. No man is exempt from work anywhere in the world. I sometimes think he is fortunate if he has to work only with his hands and not with his head. It is very easy to do what other people give you to do, but it is very difficult to give other people things to do. We cannot exempt you from work; we cannot exempt you from the strife and the heartbreaking

burden of the struggle of the day—that is common to mankind everywhere. We cannot exempt you from the loads you
must carry; we can only make them light by the spirit in
which they are carried. That is the spirit of hope, it is the
spirit of liberty, it is the spirit of justice.

When I was asked, therefore, by the Mayor and the
committee that accompanied him to come up from Washington to meet this great company of newly admitted citizens I
could not decline the invitation. I ought not to be away from
Washington, and yet I feel that it has renewed my spirit as an
American.

In Washington men tell you so many things every day
that are not so, and I like to come and stand in the presence
of a great body of my fellow-citizens, whether they have been
my fellow-citizens a long time or a short time, and drink, as
it were, out of the common fountains with them and go back
feeling that you have so generously given me the sense of
your support and of the living vitality in your hearts, of its
great ideals which made America the hope of the world.

Cultural Identity Is a Source of Pride

Patsy T. Mink

At a 1971 speaking engagement held by the West Los Angeles Japanese-American Citizens League, many members of the audience were either old enough to remember the forced relocation of Japanese Americans during World War II or had actually lived through it themselves. Title II of the International Security Act of 1950, the law which had retroactively authorized the detention and internment of Japanese Americans, had only been repealed a year prior to this meeting of the Citizens League.

On this occasion, Patsy T. Mink, a popular Hawaiian politician, spoke frankly about public misconceptions surrounding Asian Americans in the United States. At a time when the war in Vietnam raised discussions of Asian humanity across the United States, Mink argued that all children of immigrants should value the history of their ancestors' homelands. In her speech, Mink dissects stereotypes about Japanese Americans and believes that Asian American children must also learn about the history of anti-Japanese racism in America. Mink asserts that "society is big enough for all of us," and those who identify themselves as Asians must take pride and strength in what makes them unique.

I would like to thank President Kanegai and the other officers and members of the West Los Angeles Japanese-American Citizens League for this opportunity to be with

Patsy T. Mink, speech delivered to the West Los Angeles Japanese-American Citizens League, Playa Del Rey, CA, November 6, 1971.

you at your thirtieth anniversary banquet and installation. I am delighted to participate in this memorable occasion.

It must be difficult to look back thirty years to 1941 and relive the pains and agonies that were inflicted upon you as citizens, unloved and unwanted in their own country of their birth. Loving this land as much as any other citizen, it is difficult to fathom the despair and fury which many must have felt, yet who fought back and within a few years had reestablished their lives and their futures. Most of us remember these years vividly. Our faith in justice was tested many times over. Our patriotism was proven by blood of our sons upon the battlefields.

Yet today, thirty years later, to many even in this room, it is only a part of our history. Our children, thirty years old and younger, cannot follow with us these memories of the forties. They tire of our stories of the past. Their life is now, today . . . tomorrow. Their youthful fervor was poured into the symbolism of the repeal of Title II of the Internal Security Act of 1950, portrayed by its title, Emergency Detention Act. That Act became law nearly ten years *after* the Japanese were evacuated from the West Coast into "relocation camps." Yet, it stood as a reminder of what could happen again. Of course, despite the successful repeal, it could happen again, as it did indeed to the Japanese-Americans who were rounded up without any statutory authority whatsoever. It was not until 1950 that Title II became law.

A Sociological Myth

It is quite evident that I am standing before an affluent group whose surface appearance does not reveal the years of struggle and doubt that have ridden behind you.

Sociologists have generally described the Japanese-Americans as an easily acculturated people who quickly assimilated the ways of their surroundings. This has always been in my view a friendly sort of jab at our cultural background, for what it has come to mean for me is a description of a conformist which I hope I am not!

I still dream that I shall be able to be a real participant in the changing scenario of opportunity for all of America. In this respect, I share the deep frustration and anguish of our youth as I see so much around us that cries out for our attention and that we continue to neglect.

Many factors have contributed towards a deepening sense of frustration about our inability to solve our problems of poverty and racial prejudice. Undoubtedly the prolonged, unending involvement in Vietnam has contributed to this sense of hopelessness. At least for our youth who must bear the ultimate burden of this war, it seems unfair that they should be asked to serve their country in this way when there are so many more important ways in which their youth and energy can be directed to meet the urgent needs at home. They view our Government as impotent to deal with these basic issues.

It is true that Congress has passed a great many civil rights laws. The fact that new, extra laws were found necessary to make it easier for some people to realize their constitutional guarantees is a sad enough commentary on the American society, but what is even worse is the fact that the majority of our people are still unready, personally, to extend these guarantees to all despite the Constitution and all the civil rights laws, and despite their protestations to the contrary.

Certainly, no one will admit his bigotry and prejudice — yet we always find ways to clothe such feelings in more presentable forms—and few will openly advocate suppression or oppression of other men, but nevertheless, it exists.

Although Congress has repealed the Emergency Detention Act, the fight for freedom is not over. We now see a new witch hunt proclaimed in which all Government employees will be examined for their memberships and organizations. It seems that we have not yet succeeded in expunging the notion that "dangerous" persons can be identified by class or group relationships and punished accordingly.

I believe that nobody can find safety in numbers—by huddling with the larger mass in hopes of being overlooked. Those who seek to suppress will always find ways to single out others. Instead, we must change the basic attitude that all must conform or be classed as renegades and radicals. Our nation was founded on the idealistic belief in individualism and pioneering spirit, and it would be tragic for our own generation to forswear that ideal for the false security of instant assimilation.

It seems to me that our society is large enough to accept a wide diversity of types and opinions, and that no group should be forced to try to conform to the image of the population as a whole. I sometimes wonder if our goal as Japanese-Americans is to be so like the White Anglo-Saxon Protestant population as to be indistinguishable from it. If so, we will obviously never succeed!

Prejudice Against Japanese-Americans

There has been and continues to be prejudice in this country against Asians. The basis of this is the belief that the Oriental is "inscrutable." Having such base feelings, it is simple to stir up public outrage against the recognition of the People's Republic of China in the United Nations, for instance, even though reasoned judgment dictates otherwise, unless of course a Yellow Communist is really worse than a Red one!

The World War II detention overnight reduced the entire population of one national origin to an enemy, stripped of property, rights of citizenship, human dignity, and due process of law, without so much as even a stifled voice of conscience among our leading scholars or civil libertarians. More recently, the Vietnam war has reinforced the view of Orientals as something less than fully human. All Vietnamese stooping in the rice fields are pictured as the enemy, subhuman without emotions and for whom life is less valuable than for us. . . .

Somehow, we must put into perspective [Secretary of State] Dean Rusk's dread of the "yellow peril" expressed as justification for a massive antiballistics missile system on the one hand, and on the other, a quest for improved relations with Peking [China]. This latter event could have a great meaning in our own lives as Japanese-Americans. We could help this country begin to deal with Asians as people. Just the other day in a beauty parlor, I heard a congressional secretary discuss China and say, "An Asian is different, you can never figure out what he's really thinking. He has so little value for life!"

Instead of seeking refuge, we should seek to identify as Asians, and begin to serve America as the means by which she can come to understand the problems of the East. Our talents have not been used in American diplomacy, I suspect, largely because we are still not trusted enough. . . .

I know that many of you are puzzled and even dismayed by actions of some of your sons and daughters who have insisted on a more aggressive role in combating the war [in Vietnam] and other evils that exist in our society. I plead with you for understanding of this Third World movement in which not only young Japanese-Americans but many minority groups are so deeply involved.

We are confronted with what seem to be many different revolutions taking place all over the world . . . the black revolution, the revolution of emerging nations, the youth revolution here and in other countries as well—and something that was even more unheard of, the priests challenging the Vatican on the most basic issues of celibacy and birth control. It is no accident that these things are all happening at the same time, for they all stem from the same great idea that has somehow been rekindled in the world, and that is the idea that the individual is important.

All of the systems of the world today have this in common: for they are mainly concerned with industrialization, efficiency, and gross national product; the value of Man is forgotten.

The children of some of you here tonight are involved in the great protests of today—are they chronic malcontents and subversives? I think not—I think they are probably fairly well-educated, thoughtful people who see certain conditions they don't like and are trying to do something about it. I'm not sure they know exactly what they want to do. I do know they are clearly dissatisfied with the way their world has been run in the past.

So, the problem is not what to do about dissent among our young people—the problem is what to do about the causes of this dissent. The question is not "how to suppress the dissent" but how to make it meaningful . . . how to make it productive of a better society which truly places high value on individual human beings *as* human beings and not merely as so many cogs in the great, cold and impersonal machinery of an industrialized society.

I, for one, believe that the grievances of our youth are real and that they are important. Merely because the majority of students are not involved . . . merely because the dissidents are few . . . should not minimize the need for serious efforts to effectuate change. Our eighteen-year-olds now have the right to vote. Whether we like it or not, we will have to take better account of their wishes. Their acceptance as adults will bring into policy making eleven million new voters next year. Their cause for identity must be encouraged.

A Link with the Past

Our sons and daughters seek to establish a link with the past. They want to discover who they are, why they are here, and where their destinies are to take them. So many of our children are growing up in complete isolation in a society that places a premium on conformity, in middle-class homes where parents still want to play down their differences, and prefer to homogenize with society. Some of these children are rebelling and are seeking ways to preserve their uniqueness and their special heritage. I see pride and strength in this.

One of the most promising avenues for this renewed search for one's heritage is in our school systems—the logical place for instructing children in the knowledge they need. Programs of Ethnic Heritage Studies are needed in our schools. I feel that this would be particularly valuable in Hawaii, California and other areas where there are large numbers of children of Oriental descent.

It seems to me that we as Asians have a large stake in encouraging and promoting such a program. We cannot and must not presume knowledge about Asia merely because we are Asians. This requires concentrated study and dedicated determination. Of course, we do not need to become scholars cloistered in the ivory tower of some campus. We need to become aware of the enormous history of Asia and through our daily lives, regardless of what our profession, translate it to all the people with whom we deal. We have not fully met our responsibility to educate the public about Asia and its people.

I hope that all Japanese-American organizations and others with strong beliefs in the magnificent history and culture of the Orient will now help lead the way to a more enlightened America. We have an immense story to tell, for as I have said the public at large too often assumes that all civilization is Western and no worth is given to the human values of the East. As long as this belief persists, we will have future Vietnams. The way to counteract it is to build public knowledge, through school courses, travel, and dedicated emphasis on increased communications, so that our people will know and appreciate all that is Asian.

Last Thursday night in a display of utter ignorance and contempt for diversity, the House of Representatives killed the ethnic heritage studies program by a vote of 200 ayes to 159 noes. And so you see, I speak of an urgent matter. We are so few and they who do not care to understand us are so numerous.

It is fine for all citizens to pursue the good life and worldly goods on which our society places such emphasis, but there is increasing recognition that all will be ashes in our mouths unless our place as individuals is preserved. This is what the young are seeking—and I am among those who would rejoice in their goals.

They need the guidance and support of their parents to succeed, but in any event with or without us, they are trying. It behooves us to do all we can to accept their aspirations, if not all of their actions, in the hope that this new generation will be able to find a special role for themselves in America, to help build her character, to define her morality, to give her a depth in soul, and to make her realize the beauty of our diverse society with many races and cultures of which we are one small minority.

Toward a Common Identity

Linda Chavez

Conservative newspaper columnist Linda Chavez served as an educational consultant to the administration of President Ronald Reagan and in 1983 directed the U.S. Commission on Civil Rights. Author of *Out of the Barrio: Toward a New Politics of Hispanic Assimilation,* Chavez is an often outspoken critic of multiculturalism policies, especially in education. According to Chavez, communities, not the government, should be responsible for instructing America's youth in foreign cultural heritage.

In this 1992 speech Chavez reiterates how although the teaching and remembrance of cultural traditions within a family is desirable, the priority for immigrants in the United States, especially those in the school system, should be assimilation.

The face of America is changing—becoming more diverse and complex than at any time in our history. We're no longer a white-and-black society struggling to integrate two major groups of people who have been in this country for nearly four hundred years, but a multiracial, multiethnic society in which newcomers are arriving in record numbers every day. The 1980s will be remembered as a period of one of the highest levels of immigration in our nation's history. Some ten million persons immigrated to the United States in the last decade, a number as great as that of the peak decade, 1900 to 1910.

Linda Chavez, speech delivered at the National Trust for Historic Preservation Conference, Miami, FL, October 1992. Copyright © 1992 by Linda Chavez. Reproduced by permission.

Unlike the immigrants of the early part of this century who were primarily from Europe, the great bulk of the last decade's immigrants—approximately eighty percent—were from Asia and Latin America. Much has been made of this phenomenon and many who favor restricting immigration suggest that these new Asian and Latin immigrants will be less successfully absorbed into the fabric of American society: "I know that earlier large waves of immigrants didn't 'overturn' America," says former Colorado governor Dick Lamm, "but there are . . . reasons to believe that today's migration is different from earlier flows."

Hispanic Assimilation

But, in fact, when we look at one of these groups, we find that most Hispanics are assimilating the social, educational, economic, and language norms of this society despite the image of Hispanics portrayed in the media and perpetuated by Hispanic leaders. Let me just acquaint you with a few facts about the Hispanic population with which you may not be familiar:

• Mexican-origin men have the highest labor-force participation rates of any group, including non-Hispanic whites and Asians.

• U.S.-born Hispanics have rapidly moved into the middle class. The earnings of Mexican-American men are now roughly eighty percent of those of non-Hispanic white men.

• Mexican-Americans with thirteen to fifteen years of education earn, on an average, ninety-seven percent of the average earnings of non-Hispanic white males.

• Most differences in earnings between Hispanics and non-Hispanics can be explained by educational differences between the two groups, but at the secondary-school level, young Mexican-Americans are closing the gap with their non-Hispanic peers. Seventy-eight percent of second-generation Mexican-American men aged twenty-five to thirty-four have completed twelve years of school or more, compared with approximately ninety percent of comparable non-Hispanic whites.

• English proficiency is also key to earnings among Hispanics, but here, too, conventional wisdom about Hispanics is mostly invalid. The overwhelming majority of U.S.-born Hispanics are English-dominant, and one half of all third generation Mexican-Americans—like most other American ethnics—speak only one language: English.

• What's more, Hispanics, with the exception of Puerto Ricans, have marriage rates comparable to those of non-Hispanic whites. Three quarters of Mexican-origin, Cuban, and Central and South American Hispanics live in married-couple households. And nearly half own their own homes.

If these facts come as a surprise to you, it's largely because most of the analysis of Hispanics fails to note that nearly half of the adult Hispanic population is foreign-born. And like new immigrants of the past, Hispanic immigrants will take at least one generation to move up the economic ladder and into the cultural mainstream.

Immigration History

Perhaps a little history lesson is in order. The current period is not the time in our history during which we have viewed new immigrants with distrust and suspicion. We tend to forget that Italians, Greeks, Jews, Poles, and others—whom some people lump together as "Europeans"—were considered alien to the white Americans of the early twentieth century, most of whom were of British, German, or Scandinavian descent. As Thomas Sowell recounts in his book, *Ethnic America:*

> The remarkable achievements—especially intellectual achievements—of later generations of Jews cannot simply be read back into the immigrants' generation. These children often had serious educational problems. A 1910 survey of a dozen cities found two thirds of the children of Polish Jews to be below the normal grade for their ages.

Jews weren't the only group that suffered such educational disadvantages. More than half of the immigrants from southern Italy at the turn of the century could neither read nor write, nor could nearly forty percent of those from Lithuania. Nor were these "Europeans" insulated from prejudice and discrimination. For anyone who believes that immigrants of an earlier day lived in halcyon time of tolerance and acceptance among their fellow white European-descended Americans, I recommend a few hours of reading through the reports of the 1921 Dillingham Commission, which in 1924 ultimately recommended a quota system to keep out southern and eastern European immigrants and Asians.

The point is that immigrants have never had it particularly easy in this society, nor have they always been welcomed with open arms, despite Emma Lazarus's words on the base of the Statue of Liberty. Nonetheless, most of those who came here from other countries found the struggle worth the effort. And these groups did, by and large, succeed in America. Today, Italians, Jews, Poles, Greeks, and others of southern and eastern European background are virtually indistinguishable from so-called native-stock Americans on measure of earnings, status, and education. Even Chinese- and Japanese-Americans, who were subject to much greater discrimination than southern and eastern Europeans, have done exceedingly well and outperform most other groups on all indicators of social and economic success. But it took three generations for most of these groups to achieve this status. For Italian-Americans, for example, it took until 1970 before they achieved the same average educational attainment as other Americans—some sixty years after the peak of their immigration to the United States.

Past Mistakes

Is it possible, then, simply to mimic what we did in the past in treating this generation of newcomers? No. Let me concede that we did a great deal of wrong in the past, and immigrants succeeded in spite of, not because of, our mistakes. It would be neither compassionate nor legal to return to a system in which we put non-English-speaking children into public-school classrooms in which the instruction was entirely in English and expect those children to "sink or swim." In 1974 this approach was declared by the United States Supreme Court to violate our civil rights laws. Nor should we harken back to the "good old days" when Anglo conformity was the sole acceptable cultural model. But in trying to right past wrongs, we should be careful not to reverse ourselves 180 degrees by attempting to educate each group of immigrant children in their own native language and inculcate them in their own native culture. There is something wrong when two thirds of children from Spanish-speaking homes are taught to read in Spanish when they enter first grade in American public schools and three fourths are given Spanish oral-language development. If we insist on separate language instruction for all immigrant students—167 different languages are spoken in New York alone—we will close the door on integration, divide ourselves along cultural/linguistic lines, and thereby perpetuate inequalities rather than eradicate them. It seems to me that too often those who propose multicultural education are so obsessed with the excesses of Anglo conformity that they fail to see the benefits of a shared, common culture—not entirely white, Anglo-Saxon, and Protestant—but common nonetheless. And they fail to see the dangers in substituting one orthodoxy with another, no less rigid.

Political Inheritance

The more diverse we become racially and ethnically, the more important it is that we learn to tolerate differences—and also to celebrate what we all have in common. Whether we came to the United States voluntarily or involuntarily, we all choose to live here now. And more people want to live here than anywhere else in the world. No other country accepts as many immigrants as we do. Surely, even those who criticize our so-called Eurocentric society must admit that it has something to offer or there would not be such long lines of those waiting to get in—very few of them European, by the way. What is it we have that these Mexicans, Cambodians, Ethiopians, Filipinos, and others want? Two things primarily: economic opportunity and political freedom. The two, by the way, go hand in hand, and it is our legal and political institutions that protect both. Now it so happens that those political institutions did not, in fact, develop in Asia or Latin America or Africa or even throughout most of Europe. It happens that the framework for our political institutions comes from England. The basis for American jurisprudence comes from English common law—not from Spanish adaptations of Roman Law that governed most of Latin America, or from the legendary rulers of China or from the Hsia Dynasty or from Confucianism, or from the Ghanian Empire, the Kush state in Nubia, or from Mali. That is not to say that these others are not important civilizations deserving recognition in their own right, but it is to acknowledge the special importance to our particular political/legal system of the Magna Carta, habeas corpus, and trial by jury, all of which were handed down directly from England. Of course, not all of these concepts were totally indigenous to England; King Henry II adapted from the Franks the system of trial by jury to replace the oath, the ordeal, or the duel, which were used in both criminal and civil cases until the twelfth century.

In our zeal to tell the stories of other civilizations, to include the history of those whose ancestors came from places other than England, we should not attempt to rewrite the history of our own founding and our political antecedents. Nor should we blush at the thought that this political/institutional history now belongs to children who come here from Mexico, Vietnam, or Ghana or whose parents came from those countries. These children are now American children, and this is their political inheritance as much as it is the inheritance of the child of Italian or Greek or Russian roots, certainly every bit as much as it is the child of English roots. I believe that in our zeal to promote diversity we are forgetting that what makes this country virtually unique in the world is that we have forged an identity as a people even though most of us share very little in common in terms of our own personal histories. There is nothing wrong with holding onto personal history, but—given the incredible diversity of the country as a whole—it becomes increasingly difficult to expect the state to try to pass on that sense of personal history to each and every group. The most that can be expected, I think, is that we make sure that we recognize the contributions each group—once here—has made to the common history of this nation. . . .

Education Policy

The American public school was created on the premise that it would be a common school, one for all children. It has not always lived up to that ideal—certainly not before 1954—but that does not mean we should abandon the ideal. The face of America is changing, but we should not give up on the idea that we are one people, one nation. Our efforts should be dedicated to making that ideal a reality.

Is there no place, then, for the preservation of language and culture for those among new immigrants—or any others in this society—who wish to retain aspects of their former traditions? Of course there is. Some would have us believe that assimilation means that every group will be stripped of what makes it unique and that the American character will be forged into a colorless alloy in an indifferent melting pot. But, of course, that is not what has happened in this country. As a trip into the heart of any American city will tell you, ethnic communities are alive and well, even as their inhabitants enjoy the fruits of social, political, and economic integration.

The question is not whether any ethnic group has the right to maintain its language, culture, and traditions, but whose responsibility it is to do so: Is it the individual's or the group's responsibility? Or should it be the responsibility of government to ensure that each group's separate traditions be maintained? This, of course, is the heart of the debate now raging in many circles—a debate in which I come down solidly on the side of personal responsibility. If Hispanics, Asians, Jews, Greeks, or the members of any other group wish to maintain their individual and unique cultures, languages, or traditions, it must be up to them to do so. Indeed, many groups have been quite successful in preserving their native languages and cultures within the United States. Chinese parents send their children to school on Saturday to learn Cantonese or Mandarin and the history of their ancestors. Jewish children frequently attend Hebrew classes and receive religious instruction that teaches them not only the tenets of their faith but also the history of their people. Greek Americans are among the most successful of any group in maintaining their language in the United States; according to the 1980 census a majority of Greek Americans say they still speak Greek in their homes at least occasionally.

Those Hispanics who wish to maintain their native language and culture—and polls show that a majority of Hispanic immigrants do—should follow the example of their fellow ethnic Americans by establishing their own cultural societies by which to do so. Frankly, given the tremendous diversity within the Hispanic community, the only successful way for each group to ensure that its members know its history and traditions is to undertake that education itself. If government is entrusted with the responsibility, it is likely to amalgamate and homogenize in ways that make the original culture virtually indecipherable. The government, after all, is capable of lumping all twenty-two million Hispanics in this nation into one category—a category that includes Cakchikel Indians from Guatemala, mestizos from Mexico, the descendants of Italian immigrants from Argentina, Japanese immigrants from Peru, Spaniards from Europe, and the descendants of colonists who settled the Southwest nearly four hundred years ago. Wouldn't it be better to entrust each of these very different groups with the responsibility of maintaining its own traditions without the interference—or assistance—of the government?

Some critics warn that the United States is in danger of fragmenting into competing racial and ethnic groups. Historian Arthur Schlesinger, Jr., has called it the "disuniting of America." No doubt, our task is more complicated today than at any time in the recent past. Nonetheless, I remain optimistic that we can—if we commit ourselves—successfully integrate the more than seventy million blacks, Hispanics, Asians, and American Indians into our society. That we can create a new *unum* out of the many already here and the many more who are to come. But to do so will require the cooperation of us all—those who have been here for generations as well as those who are coming each day. It will require that each of us recognizes the covenant that exists between the old and the new: that we respect the rights of individuals to maintain what is unique in their ancestral heritages, but that we understand that our future is in forging a common identity of shared values and beliefs essential to the democratic ideal.

GREAT
SPEECHES
IN
HISTORY

The Impact
of
Immigration

The Immigrant and Social Unrest

Jane Addams

Nobel Prize–winning social activist Jane Addams was a pioneer in the fight to improve the lives of immigrants and the destitute in America. Addams dedicated her life to struggles for social justice, and some of those who benefited from her assistance were immigrants from the slums of Chicago. Addams helped to establish the Immigrants' Protective League and also helped found the National Federation of Settlements and Neighborhood Centers to assist these people in their adjustment to life in the United States. Most notably, she worked as an intermediary between the often-misunderstood ethnic poor and their working-class neighbors.

In this speech delivered to the 47th annual National Conference on Social Work held in 1920, Addams reminds her audience that immigrants are hard-working people with as much value for human life as native-born citizens. Americans have nothing to fear from their immigrant neighbors, she asserts, and they should most certainly not be blamed for incidences of social unrest.

I should like to begin tonight by reminding you that the world is full of social unrest of which the immigrant is more acutely conscience and perhaps understands better than do native-born Americans. We forget that there are redistributions in land, recognition of peasant proprietorship

Jane Addams, speech delivered to the National Conference on Social Work, Cincinnati, OH, June 1920.

continually being carried on in the various countries of Europe, not only those in which actual revolutions have taken place as in Hungary and Russia, but in other countries such as Roumania where there has been no violent revolution and in less well known lands where social changes are constantly taking place. . . .

They are all also terribly worried about untoward experiences which may have befallen their kinsfolk in these remote countries. For five years many of them have heard nothing directly from their families and they are wrung to the heart over the possible starvation of their parents and brothers and sisters, sometimes of their wives and children. For weeks and months and years, for instance, some of them have not been able to hear from Eastern Poland. They know of the historic events, but they have gotten no news concerning the particular people who are dear to them. They are now beginning to get letters from Hungary, but still nothing is coming out of Russia, so that many Eastern immigrants are disturbed and very unhappy for these purely human reasons. . . .

Concern for Their Homelands

On the other hand they are eager, these Poles, and Bohemians, and Croatians, to be called by their new names. They are keenly alive to the fresh start made in Poland, in Czecho-Slovakia, in Jugo-Slavia, and they are quite conscious of the great happenings in Eastern and Southern Europe.

A little while ago in a mine in Northern California, a manager noted a growing disturbance among the Slav employees. He grew nervous, as he saw the miners dividing into two camps, which were given over to much ardent discussion. He made up his mind to send for the State Militia but before he did so, a man arrived from the State Immigration Commission of California, who spoke various languages. He discovered that the miners were not planning an I.W.W. [International Workers of the World] uprising, or anything of that sort, but were divided in regard to the candidate for the presidency of the new Jugo-Slav Republic. For the moment, their minds were far from wages and hours and conditions of work, so fully were their spirits back in the old country.

Many immigrants are exhibiting that absolute absorption in regard to things that are happening over seas. In the Senate it was recently stated that one and a half million European immigrants had applied for return passports. In addition to those who wished to aid their families were those who hoped to have part in the re-distribution of land. There are many who want to go back to work out the things there which they had hoped to attain when they came to this country. But, for whatever reason they have made application, they cannot go to many of these countries, and their enforced retention constantly makes for unrest. . . .

Scapegoating Immigrants

There is a great deal more which might be said . . . from the immigrant's point of view, but let us for a moment turn to the American's point of view in regard to the immigrant and social unrest. Let us remember there has been almost no immigration to this country during the [First] World War, and that the immigrants now with us have been here at least for the five years duration of that war. In what situation do they find themselves after this period of life in America. They are feeling, some of them with good reason, that they are being looked upon with suspicion and regarded as different from the rest of the world; that whatever happens in this country that is disagreeable and hard to understand is put off upon them, as if they alone were responsible. They feel that they are now being watched in quite a new way for doing the very things they have been doing for many years without any question. I have lived in an immigrant community for more than thirty years. The people of foreign birth in that neighborhood have always held meetings, have always discussed new methods of social adjustment, and have often urged a reorganization of the social order itself. No harm has come from that. On the contrary, I can remember young men who met together at Hull House and in other halls in Chicago, twenty and thirty years ago, and made statements that the authorities today would not allow them to make, who have turned out to be prosperous citizens, thoroughly bourgeois and some of them a little too conservative. Several of these eloquent young men grown older are now in Congress. We do not want young people to be too sure that this world is already just right, or the world would never advance at all. If they discuss its reformation, it is inevitable that they should occasionally say very radical things, but if a man, as the English say, is not a little too radical when he is young, he will be much too reactionary when he is old. But if the immigrants now hold meeting and say the things they are accustomed to say, they are likely to be arrested and even deported. They cannot understand it; they do not know why they should now be treated so differently and they are puzzled and irritated. It really does seem that we are falling back into the old habit of judging men, not by their individual merits or capacities, but that we are thrusting them back into the old categories of race and religion; that we designate them by the part of the world in which they were born and then feel justified in judging them in the mass. Most immigrants have come to America because they wanted more opportunity for themselves and their children; because they believed that this was a land of freedom and equality. It is a grave matter to wilfully destroy the ideal with which they came to us, the ideal that is in the hearts of thousands of people still on the other side, who once wanted to come over here, but who are now hesitating and perhaps will never come, because they are convinced that they will find more opportunity in other lands. American manufacturers are already beginning to say that they want more labor; that we cannot allow one and a half million people to return to Europe, because American industry needs them, but after all, human labor depends upon many things. If this country ceases to offer opportunities for free development, a certain type of immigrant will cease to come and we will lose more than his labor power. We will lose an idealism and a vitality which is very much needed.

We Should Not Fear Immigrants

Sometimes when I hear Russians say, "I used to dream constantly of America, and of the time I might come here, but now I go about with the same longing in my heart for Russia, and am homesick to go back to her." We do not like to hear a man say that, for we would rather believe that America gives him his greatest opportunity for free development.

Why are we so suspicious and timid in regard to the immigrants of a type we have long had with us, and who has never brought us to grief? After the French Revolution, England passed through the same reactionary period we are now having here. England then feared the doctrines of the French Revolutionists, as we now fear Bolshevism. They enacted many oppressive and restrictive laws, thereby halting the social progress of England for decades, because later, of course, England was obliged to get rid of these measures before its development could proceed in an orderly manner and much energy was consumed in breaking down the barriers. Apparently that is the way in which the Anglo-Saxon mind takes the revolutions of others.

They Are Like Us

I beg of you, let us get back into simple human relationships with these men and women who have come to our shores and are surprisingly like the rest of us. They come with great hopes and work hard to secure a better future for their children. Some of them fail and some of them succeed, and all become modified day by day, as they live with their neighbors, according to the good will, justice and even-handed enforcement of the law which surrounds them all. Nothing so produces social unrest as a sense of injustices, a conviction that the law is unfairly enforced.

To this group of social workers, many of whom are closely identified with immigrant interests, I should like to say,—"Re-assure your neighbors as best you may. Tell them that this day will pass. That America will again come to regard them as simple friends and neighbors."

Economic Well-Being Depends on Tolerance

Eric A. Johnston

Eric A. Johnston believes that racial and class divisions in American society weaken the economy and threaten individual freedoms. In this frequently referenced address Johnston delivered to the Writers' War Board in 1945, Johnston argues against intolerance of foreigners and newcomers to America's shores. According to Johnston, the wide variety of races that form U.S. citizenry strengthen the nation's economy and its character, and this diaspora of people politically and financially contribute to the wealth of the United States. Furthermore, intolerance of immigrants and foreigners threatens capitalist productivity and national security.

Your subject tonight is "The Myth That Threatens America." Surely, the business man and the artist share responsibility in eradicating the myth of group or class superiority. Those who pretend that it does not exist are kidding themselves.

Of all the social problems that face our great country in this era of crisis, that of national unity seems to me the most challenging. Most other problems will not be solved if the American people are divided into mutually hostile and suspicious groups, sections and classes. More than that; even if solutions were possible under such conditions, they would

Eric A. Johnston, speech delivered to the Writers' War Board, New York, NY, January 11, 1945.

hardly be worth achieving. They would be empty victories, utterly meaningless, if the character of our American civilization were changed in the process.

And the core of that civilization, it seems to me, is in the sacred dignity of the human being, regardless of race or class or place of birth. Individual freedom—liberty within a framework of law—is essential to the America we know and love. Without these elements it would no longer be *our* America, except in the geographical sense. In the deeper moral sense it would be an alien country, where those of us who cherish ideals of freedom would be exiles in our own homes.

Preserving America

We are all of us, in our several ways, seeking to preserve America. Millions of our sons are doing it on battlefields [of World War II] with bombs and bayonets. You who write and inspire and propagandize do it with the weapon of words. Those of us who build and manufacture do it with machines and goods. But what all of us have in mind is not simply the physical preservation of our country. It is the preservation of those human values which are implicit in the word America—the freedom, the opportunities, the equalities, the democratic ideals celebrated in our national songs and poetry and books and holiday speeches.

I know there are the clichés of American patriotism and after-dinner oratory. But we do not discount them for that reason. On the contrary, we accept them and cherish them as proof positive that the American Dream is a dream of free men living together in a spirit of harmony and trust.

I regard as profoundly significant the fact that the average American, whether he be a blasé business man or a cynical writer, looks on these so-called clichés as desirable even when he doesn't live up to them. Equally significant is the fact that even the salesmen of dissension must disguise their sales talks in the phraseology of American freedom.

Race hatreds and group intolerance simply do not jibe with any of the formulas of freedom so dear to the American heart. To the extent they are allowed to flourish, they threaten to change the American Dream into another European nightmare.

Let's not underestimate the threat. There is a tendency to soft-pedal the spread of alien doctrines of intolerance. The theory, I suppose, is that the best way to treat a disease is to pretend that it doesn't exist. That is a cowardly theory and worse, a futile one. It seems to me that honest diagnosis is the first and indispensable measure in meeting the challenge of propagandas and whispering campaigns directed against foreigners, against Jews, against Catholics, against Negroes.

Equally dangerous, but not so dramatic, and therefore not so well understood, are the campaigns of intolerance and vilification that are directed against economic groups such as business, labor and agriculture—sometimes by one another, and sometimes by the enemies of one or all. To the extent that business has been guilty of such intolerance in any direction I deplore it. I have set my face against it, and I shall continue to denounce it. To the extent that you, as writers have been guilty of this same type of intolerance with respect to any of these groups, including business, I invite you to have another look to see if the beam in your eye has gotten you off the beam of tolerance.

I have been privileged to travel widely in our country, and I do not hesitate to offer my personal testimony that the tremendous tension of race and group animosities is warping the very foundations of American democratic life. Men and women who should know better—who do know better—allow themselves to mouth the catch phrases of anti-Semitism and anti-foreignism, of anti-business, or anti-labor, anti-farm. Most of them are not themselves aware that they have been infected by the virus of intolerance which already has the whole world writhing in the fatal fever of war.

When there's a riot in Detroit or Harlem, when racial antagonisms break into the open in Boston or Brooklyn, it's more comfortable to shrug them off as local incidents. But the truth must be faced. These episodes of violence are symptoms of pressures and emotions and maladjustments which are nation-wide.

The first thing we must do, it seems to me, is to confront the reality. Obviously the most violent and deep seated of our antipathies are racial and religious. Widespread though these expressions of group hatred are, it is a hopeful fact that they still afflict only a small minority of the American population. That minority can be curbed and re-educated if conscious and organized efforts are undertaken.

At the very worst, that minority can be frightened into desisting. Not by legal threats—you can't legislate the golden rule as you can the gold standard. I mean that Americans can be made sharply aware that intolerance endangers not merely the small groups against whom it is directed but the country as a whole. The obstreperous hate-mongers and their foolish or frivolous fellow travelers who think it is smart to rock the American boat may drown with the other passengers. . . .

Economic Dangers

Viewed from the narrowest vantage point of the nation's well-being, quite aside from human and moral considerations, the growth of doctrines of race and group hatreds represents a major economic threat. America has prospered because it has provided avenues of economic expression to all men who had the urge and the capacity to advance themselves. Wherever we erect barriers on the grounds of race or religion, or of occupational or professional status, we hamper the fullest expansion of our economic society. Intolerance is destructive. Prejudice produces no wealth. Discrimination is a fool's economy.

Freedom of the individual is the most vital condition for creative life in economy as in every other department of human existence. Such freedom is impossible where men are restricted by reason of race or origin, on the one hand, or on the other, paralyzed by fears and hatreds of their neighbors.

There are some in our country—industrialists, white collar workers, laboring people—who hold to the myth that economic progress can be attained on the principle of an unbalanced seesaw. They think that if some groups can be forever held *down*, the others will forever enjoy economic privileges and prosperity at the end which is up.

Fortunately it does not work that way. Any advantage thus gained must be paid for out of the fruits of the productive plant. The withholding of jobs and business opportunities from some people does not make more jobs and business opportunities for others. Such a policy merely tends to drag down the whole economic level. You can't sell an electric refrigerator to a family that can't afford electricity. Perpetuating poverty for some merely guarantees stagnation for all. True economic progress demands that the whole nation move forward at the same time. It demands that all artificial barriers erected by ignorance and intolerance be removed. To put it in the simplest terms, we are all in business together. Intolerance is a species of boycott and any business or job boycott is a cancer in the economic body of the nation. I repeat: Intolerance is destructive. Prejudice produces no wealth. Discrimination is a fool's economy.

The Duty of the Media

These are things that should be made manifest to the American people if we are to counteract the pestiferous labors of race and group hate-mongers. The job lies to a large extent in the hands of you writers, in your colleagues in the movies, the theater, radio, the press. You are the people with direct access to the mind—and what is more important, to the heart and emotions—of the American people.

You must somehow take words like freedom and democracy and unity and lift them to the level of religious fervor. We require more than a broad acceptance of these American concepts. We need an eager enthusiasm. And you, in particular, have the power to arouse it and to keep it alive. I want to emphasize that.

If eternal vigilance is the price of liberty, the writer and the artist generally have a prime duty in keeping the vigil. It is for them to dramatize the strength and beauty that resides in America's multiplicity of races, religions, national origins and social backgrounds. The totalitarians who looked on us as "mongrels," as a chaos of clashing cultures, have learned their mistake. We always must remember that America is a nation made up of the peoples of all lands.

Any metallurgist will tell you that the toughest, most resistant metals are not "pure" ores but alloys that blend the most valuable qualities of many ores. It is thus with the American, who fuses in his blood and his spirit the virtues and vitalities of many races, creeds, and cultures—giving us an amalgam that is new, unique, and immeasurably strong.

That is why tolerance is necessarily and rightly a supreme American characteristic. In truth, we must continue to cultivate our native American tolerance for everything except intolerance.

Our enemies have learned in this war the toughness of our fiber. It now remains for the American people, likewise, to absorb that lesson. It was [poet] Walt Whitman who celebrated the diversity that is America's strength. "This is not a nation," he proclaimed, "but a teaming of nations." In some measure every poet sensitive to the nature of our still young American experiment has felt and expressed that diversity. Russell Davenport has just done it in "My Country." Perhaps the poet, more than the economist or historian, senses the absurdity in attempts to hammer all Americans into a single national type and discriminate against the minorities who do not conform to an arbitrary creation.

Let's not apologize for the amazing variety of our human material here in America. Let us rather glory in it as the source of our robust spirit and opulent achievements. Let's not deny that there are differences in race and that our country has all the fifty-seven varieties of God's humanity. Let us merely make clear that these differences cannot be measured on any scale of good, better and best. They are all equally valid and all must continue to contribute to the magnificent mosaic of American life.

Immigrant Contributions

Subtract from the grand total of America the contributions of our racial and religious and economic minorities—and what remains? Subtract foreign-born Andrew Carnegie from our metallurgical industry; or David Sarnoff from American radio; or George Gershwin and the Negro composers from our native music; or Norwegian-born Knute Rockne from our football; or Dutch-born Edward William Bok from publishing; or Danish-born William S. Knudsen from the automotive industry; or Russian-born Major de Seversky from American aviation; or Belgian-born Leo H. Baekeland from

American chemical achievements; or slave-born Dr. George Washington Carver from biological developments. The temptation is to list hundreds and thousands who have thrown their particular genius into the American melting pot.

And behind those whose names we know are the nameless legions of immigrants, generation after generation, whose labor and lives went into every bridge, and tunnel, every mine and factory in these United States.

Too many Americans—indeed, too many of the immigrants themselves, whatever their race or land of birth—behave as if America only *gave* things to newcomers. We need to be reminded that America *received* more than it gave. After all, our country let the strangers in because it needed their muscle power, their purchasing power, their fecundity and their brains.

It is this vision of a society wonderfully rounded by reason of its many racial contributions—of an *inter*nation within the borders of a vast nation—that should be brought home to every American child and adult. The cooperation of these multiple elements—the unity of a powerful amalgam—has given a peculiar destiny and genius to our country. In pointing out our achievements to our preachers of division and distrust we are protecting that part of our history that still lies in the future.

But it seems to me that all of us who fight against intolerance can hurt our own cause by expecting too much too soon. The simple human fact is that prejudice is latent in all of us. The average Protestant, Catholic, Jew is normally prejudiced in favor of his own kind and against the others. The underprivileged are prejudiced against the well-to-do. The strong are prejudiced against the weak and vice versa. Men are prejudiced against women and women, alas, are even more prejudiced against men. The saintly soul who goes through life devoid of all prejudices is rare indeed.

These attitudes cannot be wished away or talked away or smothered with fine phrases. They are the products of centuries of history which must be taken into account in any functioning society. . . .

I know that the physical ingredients for a better, a happier and nobler America are at our disposal. Raw materials, machinery, skills, manpower in abundance. Can we match these with intelligence, good-will, social idealism and tolerance?

In the perspective of history, it will appear that ours is the tragic privilege—the tragic privilege of living in the greatest military crisis since Napoleon, the greatest economic crisis since Adam Smith, the greatest moral crisis since the fall of the Roman Empire. But if ours is the tragic privilege, history will also show that ours is the magnificent opportunity—the magnificent opportunity to understand that in unity there is strength; in good-will there is prosperity; in tolerance there is progress—progress towards a better, a healthier and a happier America. In fact, this is the only way we may have peace at home or abroad in our lifetime.

Illegal Immigration Policy Must Be Humane

Antonia Hernández

Controversial California Proposition 187 gathered nationwide attention with its broad restrictions that were designed to combat the influx of Mexican immigrants into the United States. The measure that would have barred undocumented immigrants from public education and social services, and denied them medical attention passed in November 1994 but was ultimately held up by a federal court. One effect of the initiative was to inspire a national dialogue on immigration, with highly charged opinions on either side.

In this argument civil rights attorney Antonia Hernández, president of the Mexican American Legal Defense and Educational Fund (MALDEF), explains her opposition to Proposition 187. She argues that it would hurt both the underrepresented victims and the California taxpayers who would pay for it.

I mmigration—legal and illegal—is an inherently difficult and complex issue that defies simplistic and reactionary solutions like [California Proposition] 187.

On the one hand, I know all too well that it is easier to "crack down" on the undocumented worker, easier to punish the children of undocumented immigrants, easier to assume that aggressive posture than to deal with the root eco-

Antonia Hernández, speech delivered at the Temple Isaiah in Los Angeles, CA, October 5, 1994. Copyright © 1994 by Antonia Hernández.

nomic causes of the migration north.

There is no question that the influx has changed the dynamics of cities like Los Angeles, and its impact has been felt in Washington as surely as Sacramento.

We cannot ignore that fact.

Yet, despite all the rhetoric about undocumented immigrants living off the system, the fact is that they come to work and build a better life for themselves and their children, not to take advantage of our educational, medical, and public services. They come to share in our great American work ethic.

We know that many immigrants come from the lowest socioeconomic strata of Mexico and Central America. We know that the immigrant is no longer a male looking to work seasonally and then return to his native country. Entire families are migrating north and settling permanently.

Immigration Facts

It is therefore critical that we approach undocumented immigration with the facts.

In 1993, only 1.5 percent of immigrants received Social Security.

In 1992 the INS [Immigration and Naturalization Service] reported that 0.5 percent of undocumented immigrants received food stamps or Aid to Families with Dependent Children (AFDC) and about half had private health insurance while only 21 percent used any government health services.

According to the Urban Institute, when all levels of government are considered together, immigrants contribute more in taxes paid than in services received.

Yet in the past few years, public discourse over immigration policy, shaped by misinformation, has shifted dangerously toward extremism. The by-product of that movement has created a rise in xenophobia and the scapegoating of immigrants.

Indeed, in the past several months, we have seen the federal government approve such proposals as banning emergency aid to undocumented immigrants who were victims of the earthquake in Los Angeles, funding the unemployment benefits extension program by cutting off benefits to legal permanent residents, and consider cutting off educational benefits to undocumented children in the public schools.

So taken by the effort to deny aid to undocumented immigrants who had been victimized by the earthquake, Secretary of Housing and Urban Development Henry Cisneros was compelled to say: "It is sad that the circumstances of a disaster would result in making these kinds of distinctions about human suffering." . . .

All of these efforts are extreme and retrograde and speak to the virulence of the anti-immigrant sentiment that has gripped the state and nation.

I will tell you that I have always been averse to extremism and no less so when it comes to immigration policy.

For me, the answer lies in compassion, moderation and—above all—reason.

Proposition 187

While we all have legitimate concerns about illegal immigration, the truth is that Proposition 187 is intended to save money and solve problems but will only make the situation worse and create a host of new problems—expensive ones.

Proposition 187 does nothing to enforce the laws we already have, nor does it beef up enforcement at the borders.

Recklessly drafted, 187 violates federal laws that control federal funding to our schools and hospitals. The independent analysis of 187 in the voter pamphlet shows passage of the proposition could cost our schools and hospitals $15 billion in lost federal funds.

Let's put that staggering amount in a context that every Californian can understand. Replacing that money would necessitate a $1,600 annual tax increase for the average California family.

Proponents of the proposition claim that the state will save hundreds of millions of dollars by denying "nonemergency" medical care to the undocumented. First of all, the estimated undocumented immigrant use of the medical services that 187 would prohibit is very low, just a fraction of one percent of California's budget.

Also, refusal to provide fundamental health care is a severe danger to public interest. If 187 is successful in denying these basic services, undocumented persons will not be treated even if their medical problems are serious, even if they have communicable diseases, even if a low-cost dose of preventive medicine or an immunization could keep them from ending up in county emergency rooms with far more serious ailments that will cost the state even more to treat.

In this country, we long ago recognized that health is a community concern. Volumes of treatises on public health recognized the danger to all of society if certain diseases and injuries are left untreated. The trend toward health care reform shows above all that we believe illnesses are not confined solely to one segment of our population. Yet, under this provision children would not be immunized and persons in desperate need of medical attention will not seek such care for fear of being reported to the INS. This constitutes not just a threat to the individual but a threat to our public health. As a society, we are best protected by treating the disease, not by turning away the individual in need of care.

By imposing yet another bureaucratic procedure in providing services, the provision will increase escalating costs of publicly-funded health services. Moreover, requiring verification and denying benefits or services on the basis of suspicion could cause unnecessary, and potentially life-endangering, delays and denials of care to citizens and legal residents who are otherwise entitled to medical assistance. . . .

When you get beyond all the misinformation, you realize that undocumented immigrants are already ineligible for the vast majority of public social services such as state welfare or food stamps. One-eighty-seven's provision to deny such services to the undocumented merely creates a costly, enormous and unnecessary bureaucratic burden. Because existing federal verification procedures already prevent and discourage the undocumented from applying for public social services, the administrative costs of implementing this provision would offset, and most likely exceed any potential savings. . . .

Finally, 187 does nothing to curb unlawful immigration into the state.

As a nation, we have been too apt to forget the benefits immigrants bring. We have also been given the opportunity to heed the lessons of our immigration history, and to this day we have squandered that opportunity. Instead, we have found ourselves in a desultory discourse that appeals to our worst nature as Americans, that plays to our darkest fears of "the foreigner."

Perhaps the saddest part of it all is that in so doing we have victimized not only voiceless immigrants but ourselves. For as I look upon this room and all the many faces, I am reminded again of this nation's great good fortune—that blessing—to be inheritor of such wealth, a true common wealth.

William Saroyan once wrote: "This is America, and the only foreigners here are those who forget it is America."

There has been all too much forgetting and not enough acknowledgment of our own immigrant stories, and the debate over immigration policy must be refracted through such a multicolored prism.

For if we are unable to bring some reason and decency to this debate, what is at stake is nothing less than who we are as a people, and how we define ourselves as a nation.

In the end, however, I remain optimistic that we will find our way to dealing compassionately and thoughtfully with immigrants. We will begin to move beyond the rhetoric and misinformation and posit the solutions to an issue that defies simplistic and reactionary approaches. I am optimistic because it is not our nature as Americans to turn our backs on those in need in the wake of a disaster—undocumented immigrants or not. It is not our nature to punish children and blame the ills of a nation on a small sector of our society. It is not our nature to turn away from issues that must be dealt with.

We will find our way to a reasoned and dignified policy by adhering to the sense of humanity that has made this country great, and acknowledges the role of the government controlling our borders. I know that we are a good and decent people—that is our nature and our franchise as Americans.

Facing the Challenges of Diversity

William J. Clinton

When President William J. Clinton delivered this speech
to the Portland State University graduates at their commencement ceremony, critics of current U.S. immigration
policy seized on Clinton's demographic predictions of no
majority race in the United States within the next fifty
years.

Clinton lauds the historical contributions of immigrants, and explains how the United States is dealing with
its largest wave of immigration in more than one hundred
years. Other topics he discusses are the role of the
schools in preparing English-speaking citizens, and the
unique benefits derived from the diverse composition of
the United States. Diverse peoples enrich each other, Clinton asserts, and what binds us together is our equality in
the eyes of God.

Today, I want to talk to you about what may be the
most important subject of all—how we can strengthen
the bonds of our national community as we grow
more racially and ethnically diverse.

It was just a year ago tomorrow that I launched a national initiative on race, asking Americans to address the per-
sistent problems and the limitless possibilities of our diversity. This effort is especially important right now because, as

William J. Clinton, speech delivered at the Portland State University Commencement Ceremony, Portland, OR, June 13, 1998.

we grow more diverse, our ability to deal with the challenges will determine whether we can really bind ourselves together as one America. And even more importantly in the near-term, and over the next few years, perhaps, as well, our ability to exercise world leadership for peace, for freedom, for prosperity in a world that is both smaller and more closely connected, and yet increasingly gripped with tense, often bloody conflicts rooted in racial, ethnic and religious divisions—our ability to lead that kind of world to a better place rests in no small measure on our ability to be a better place here in the United States that can be a model for the world.

The driving force behind our increasing diversity is a new, large wave of immigration. It is changing the face of America. And while most of the changes are good, they do present challenges which demand more both from new immigrants and from our citizens. Citizens share a responsibility to welcome new immigrants, to ensure that they strengthen our nation, to give them their chance at the brass ring.

In turn, new immigrants have a responsibility to learn, to work, to contribute to America. If both citizens and immigrants do their part, we will grow ever stronger in the new global information economy.

More than any other nation on Earth, America has constantly drawn strength and spirit from wave after wave of immigrants. In each generation, they have proved to be the most restless, the most adventurous, the most innovative, the most industrious of people. Bearing different memories, honoring different heritages, they have strengthened our economy, enriched our culture, renewed our promise of freedom and opportunity for all.

Public Attitudes Toward Immigrants

Of course, the path has not always run smooth. Some Americans have met each group of newcomers with suspicion and violence and discrimination. So great was the hatred of Irish immigrants 150 years ago that they were greeted with signs that read, "No Dogs Or Irish." So profound was the fear of Chinese in the 1880s that they were barred from entering the country. So deep was the distrust of immigrants from Southern and Eastern Europe at the beginning of this century that they were forced to take literacy tests specifically designed to keep them out of America.

Eventually, the guarantees of our Constitution and the better angels of our nature prevailed over ignorance and insecurity, over prejudice and fear.

But now we are being tested again—by a new wave of immigration larger than any in a century, far more diverse than any in our history. Each year, nearly a million people come legally to America. Today, nearly one in ten people in America was born in another country; one in five schoolchildren are from immigrant families. Today, largely because of immigration, there is no majority race in Hawaii or Houston or New York City. Within five years there will be no majority race in our largest state, California. In a little more than 50 years there will be no majority race in the United States. No other nation in history has gone through demographic change of this magnitude in so short a time.

What do the changes mean? They can either strengthen and unite us, or they can weaken and divide us. We must decide.

Let me state my view unequivocally, I believe new immigrants are good for America. They are revitalizing our cities. They are building our new economy. They are strengthening our ties to the global economy, just as earlier waves of immigrants settled the new frontier and powered the Industrial Revolution. They are energizing our culture and broadening our vision of the world. They are renewing our most basic values and reminding us all of what it truly means to be an American.

It means working hard, like a teenager from Vietnam who does his homework as he watches the cash register at his family's grocery store. It means making a better life for your children, like a father from Russia who works two jobs and still finds time to take his daughter to the public library to practice her reading. It means dreaming big dreams, passing them on to your children. . . .

[Some Americans] worry that new immigrants come not to work hard, but to live off our largesse. They're afraid the America they know and love is becoming a foreign land. This reaction may be understandable, but it's wrong. It's especially wrong when anxiety and fear give rise to policies and ballot propositions to exclude immigrants from our civic life. I believe it's wrong to deny law-abiding immigrants benefits available to everyone else; wrong to ignore them as people not worthy of being counted in the census. It's not only wrong, it's un-American.

Let me be clear: I also think it's wrong to condone illegal immigration that flouts our laws, strains our tolerance, taxes our resources. Even a nation of immigrants must have rules and conditions and limits, and when they are disregarded, public support for immigration erodes in ways that are destructive to those who are newly arrived and those who are still waiting patiently to come.

Most Immigrants Contribute to Society

We must remember, however, that the vast majority of immigrants are here legally. In every measurable way, they give more to our society than they take. Consider this: On average, immigrants pay $1,800 more in taxes every year than they cost our system in benefits. Immigrants are paying into Social Security at record rates. Most of them are young, and they will help to balance the budget when we baby boomers retire and put strains on it.

New immigrants also benefit the nation in ways not so easily measured, but very important. We should be honored that America, whether it's called the City on a Hill, or the Old Gold Mountain, or El Norte, is still seen around the world as the land of new beginnings. We should all be proud that people living in isolated villages in far corners of the world actually recognize the Statue of Liberty. We should rejoice that children the world over study our Declaration of Independence and embrace its creed.

My fellow Americans, we descendants of those who passed through the portals of Ellis Island must not lock the door behind us. Americans whose parents were denied the rights of citizenship simply because of the color of their skin must not deny those rights to others because of the country of their birth or the nature of their faith.

We should treat new immigrants as we would have wanted our own grandparents to be treated. We should share our country with them, not shun them or shut them out. But mark my words, unless we handle this well, immigration of this sweep and scope could threaten the bonds of our union.

Around the world we see what can happen when people who live on the same land put race and ethnicity before country, and humanity. If America is to remain the world's most diverse democracy, if immigration is to strengthen America as it has throughout our history, then we must say to one another: whether your ancestors came here in slave ships or on the Mayflower, whether they landed on Ellis Island or at Los Angeles International Airport, or have been here for thousands of years, if you believe in the Declaration of Independence and the Constitution, if you accept the responsibilities as well as the rights embedded in them, then you are an American.

Only that belief can keep us one America in the 21st century. So I say, as President, to all our immigrants, you are welcome here. But you must honor laws, embrace our culture, learn our language, know our history; and when the time comes, you should become citizens. And I say to all Americans, we have responsibilities as well to welcome our newest immigrants, to vigorously enforce laws against discrimination. And I'm very proud that our nation's top civil rights enforcer is Bill Lam Lee, the son of Chinese immigrants who grew up in Harlem.

We must protect immigrants' rights and ensure their access to education, health care, and housing and help them to become successful, productive citizens. When immigrants take responsibility to become citizens and have met all the requirements to do so, they should be promptly evaluated and accepted.

The present delays in the citizenship process are unacceptable and indefensible. And together, immigrants and citizens alike, let me say we must recommit ourselves to the general duties of citizenship. Not just immigrants, but every American should know what's in our Constitution and understand our shared history. Not just immigrants, but every American should participate in our democracy by voting, by volunteering and by running for office. Not just immigrants, but every American, on our campuses and in our communities, should serve—community service breeds good citizenship. And not just immigrants, but every American should reject identity politics that seeks to separate us, not bring us together.

Ethnic pride is a very good thing. America is one of the places which most reveres the distinctive ethnic, racial, religious heritage of our various peoples. The days when immigrants felt compelled to Anglicize their last name or deny their heritage are, thankfully, gone. But pride in one's ethnic and racial heritage must never become an excuse to withdraw from the larger American community. That does not honor diversity; it breeds divisiveness. And that could weaken America.

Not just immigrants, but every American should recognize that our public schools must be more than places where our children learn to read, they must also learn to be good citizens. They must all be able to make America's heroes, from Washington to Lincoln to Eleanor Roosevelt and Rosa Parks and Cesar Chavez, their own.

The Role of the Public School System

Today, too many Americans, and far too many immigrant children attend crowded, often crumbling inner city schools. Too many drop out of school altogether. And with more children from immigrant families entering our country and our schools than at any time since the turn of the century, we must renew our efforts to rebuild our schools and make them the best in the world. They must have better facilities; they must have smaller classes; they must have properly trained teachers; they must have access to technology; they must be the best in the world.

All of us, immigrants and citizens alike, must ensure that our new group of children learn our language, and we should find a way to do this together instead of launching another round of divisive political fights.

In the schools within the White House—in the schools within just a few miles of the White House, across the Potomac River, we have the most diverse school district in America, where there are children from 180 different racial and ethnic groups, speaking as native tongues about 100 languages.

Now, it's all very well for someone to say, everyone of them should learn English immediately. But we don't at this time necessarily have people who are trained to teach them English in all those languages. So I say to you, it is important for children to retain their native language. But unless they also learn English, they will never reach their full potential in the United States.

Of course, English is learned at different rates, and, of course, children have individual needs. But that cannot be an excuse for making sure that when children come into our school system, we do whatever it takes with whatever resources are at hand to make sure they learn as quickly as they can the language that will be the dominant language of this country's commerce and citizenship in the future.

We owe it to these children to do that. And we should not either delay behind excuses or look for ways to turn what is essentially a human issue of basic decency and citizenship and opportunity into a divisive political debate. We have a stake together in getting together and moving forward on this.

Let me say, I applaud the students here at Portland State who are tutoring immigrant children to speak and read English. You are setting the kind of example I want our country to follow.

A Tie That Binds a Diverse Citizenry

One hundred and forty years ago, in the First Lady's hometown of Chicago, immigrants outnumbered native Americans. Addressing a crowd there in 1858, Abraham Lincoln asked what connection those immigrants could possibly feel to people like George Washington and Thomas Jefferson and John Adams, who founded our nation. Here was his answer: If they, the immigrants, look back through this history to trace their connection to those days by blood, they will find they have none. But our founders proclaimed that we are all created equal in the eyes of God. And that, Lincoln said, is the electric cord in that declaration that links the hearts of patriotic and liberty-loving people everywhere.

Well, that electric cord, the conviction that we are all created equal in the eyes of God, still links every graduate here with every new immigrant coming to our shores and every American who ever came before us. If you carry it with conscience and courage into the new century, it will light our way to America's greatest days—your days.

So, members of the class of 1998, go out and build the future of your dreams. Do it together, for your children, for your grandchildren, for your country.

Good luck, and God bless you.

Appendix of Biographies

Jane Addams

Pacifist and social reformer Jane Addams, a pioneer in the fight to improve the lives of immigrants and the destitute in America, was also known for her immense contributions to the fields of social work, feminism, and education. She was born Laura Jane Addams in Cedarville, Illinois, on September 6, 1860, to Sarah Weber Addams and John Huy Addams. When Jane was three her mother died, and her father remarried five years later. The patriarch, an abolitionist and Quaker who later became a senator from Illinois, profoundly influenced his daughter's philosophies on public service. John Addams instilled values of social justice in young Jane through his active participation in the Underground Railroad and the gatherings for liberal-minded intellectuals he hosted at his home.

Although she had wanted to go to Smith College, Addams attended her father's choice for her education, Rockford Female Seminary. Despite a spine ailment that affected both her walk and the curvature of her back, in 1881 she graduated as class valedictorian. The unexpected death of her father that same year affected her ability to continue her education and led to a period of self-reflection. She took a trip to Europe with friends, including a woman from Rockford named Ellen Gates Starr, where she was appalled to see the living conditions of the poor who lived in the slums of London. Influenced by a neighborhood center she had seen on her trip, in 1889 Addams and Starr created a settlement house for the poor immigrants who lived in the slums of Chicago, Illinois. They called the sanctuary Hull House.

At Hull House immigrants could take English classes, join youth clubs, learn a trade, and find day care for their young children. Addams herself lived at Hull House with her constituency, and there she helped other volunteers assist the disenfranchised and working poor. Addams was instrumental in establishing the Immigrants' Protective League and the National Federation of Settlements and Neighborhood Centers to assist these people in their adjustment to America. She also lectured frequently on the subject of immigration.

An accomplished author, Addams chronicled her experiences as an advocate for the poor in the slums of Chicago in *Twenty Years at Hull House*. Her many books include *Democracy and Social Ethics*, *The Spirit of Youth and the City Streets*, and *Peace and*

Bread in Time of War. In 1931 she won the Nobel Peace Prize. She died on May 21, 1935.

Pat Buchanan

Political commentator Pat Buchanan was born on November 2, 1938, in Washington, D.C. According to his autobiography, Buchanan's paternal Scotch-Irish ancestors immigrated to the United States in the late 1700s; some of them settled in the American South, and others settled in the North. His maternal ancestors were German.

In 1961 Buchanan graduated from Georgetown University with a bachelor's degree in English, and he completed his master's degree at Columbia the following year. Drawing upon his education as a journalist and the conservative values he had learned from his father, Buchanan took a job as an editorial writer for the *St. Louis Globe-Democrat*. He left the paper to obtain a broader span of influence for his political philosophies, and in 1966 he became a speechwriter for Richard Nixon. His working relationship with Nixon lasted until 1974. Buchanan left the White House after Nixon's resignation and gained national attention as a spokesperson for the ultraconservative wing of the Republican Party. He moved between journalism and politics over the next several years, eventually serving in the administrations of Presidents Gerald Ford and Ronald Reagan.

Buchanan ran for president himself in 1992 and 1996, and his (unsuccessful) campaign platforms focused largely on the issue of immigration. He currently hosts a televised talk show on political issues and runs the American Cause, an organization that opposes affirmative action, current U.S. immigration policy, gay rights, and America's participation in the United Nations.

Linda Chavez

Linda Chavez was born in Albuquerque, New Mexico, in 1947 to an English-Irish mother and Spanish father. Her father worked as a house painter, and her mother worked as a waitress and a department store clerk. Chavez first encountered racism when her family relocated to Denver. While still a teenager she became a politically active liberal who marched in opposition to segregation. Highly influenced by her conservative father, Chavez continued her education at the University of Colorado. After completing her bachelor's degree, she attended graduate classes in English literature at the University of California at Los Angeles (UCLA).

At UCLA Chavez was asked to teach a class in the emerging

field of Chicano studies. In her opinion, not enough literature existed to create a course; this put her at odds with radical students who protested her syllabus and threatened her personal safety. She left UCLA in the 1970s to edit the magazine of the American Federation of Teachers. After establishing herself as an editorialist and a spokesperson for conservative causes, Chavez served as an educational consultant to the Ronald Reagan administration and in 1983 directed the U.S. Commission on Civil Rights. During her controversial tenure, she alienated civil rights groups by opposing both affirmative action and increases in the minimum wage law.

The author of *Out of the Barrio: Toward a New Politics of Hispanic Assimilation*, Chavez is an outspoken proponent of English-only initiatives and is a critic of multiculturalism, especially in education. In 1998 she joined with millionaire Ron Unz to create the organization U.S. English in hopes of eliminating bilingual education. In 2001 she became President George W. Bush's first choice as secretary of labor, but she withdrew her name from consideration when it was revealed that she employed an illegal immigrant, a woman from Guatemala, in her household. She is currently the head of the Center for Equal Opportunity, a conservative lobbying group.

Robert H. Clancy

U.S. representative Robert Henry Clancy was born in Wayne County, Detroit, Michigan, in 1882. After majoring in English, Clancy earned his bachelor of arts degree from the University of Michigan at Ann Arbor in 1907 and stayed at the school to study law for a year. After four years as a newspaper journalist in Detroit, he began his political career by accepting a position as a congressional secretary. He later worked for the secretary of commerce, as an appraiser for U.S. customs, and served as manager of the War Trade Board in Detroit during World War I.

Congressman Clancy, who was elected as both a Democrat (1923–1925) and a Republican (1927–1933), argued against the wildly popular Johnson-Reed Act of 1924. After years of public service he joined the private sector as a manufacturing executive and retired in 1948. Clancy spent his entire life in Michigan, where he died on April 23, 1962.

William J. Clinton

William Jefferson Clinton was born in Hope, Arkansas, in 1946. Educated in the public schools of Hot Springs, Arkansas, Clinton was a top student who showed an early interest in politics. During a trip to Washington, D.C., with a political youth group called

Boys Nation, he met President John F. Kennedy; this meeting had a profound impact on the young student, who greatly admired Kennedy. After graduating from Georgetown University with a degree in international relations, Clinton enrolled in Yale Law School, where he met Hillary Rodham. The two married in 1975, and the next year he was elected attorney general for the state of Arkansas. In 1978 Clinton ran a successful campaign for governor of Arkansas and served for twelve years (from 1979 until 1981 and again from 1983 to 1992).

In 1992 Clinton, a Democrat, defeated the incumbent, Republican George H.W. Bush, and became the forty-second president of the United States. He was elected to a second term in 1996, and during his presidency the nation experienced a large surge in immigration. On June 13, 1998, Clinton delivered a speech to Portland State University graduates in which he predicted a major shift in U.S. demographics—no majority race in the United States within the next fifty years. Some opponents of current immigration policies refer to this speech with disdain and suggest that Clinton's implication was that Anglo-Americans, the historical majority population, needed to be pulled from dominance. These critics believe that Clinton-era multiculturalism was a dangerous policy trend that would change the traditional character of the nation.

Critics of Clinton and his administration were elated after the 1996 scandal involving intern Monica Lewinsky led to his impeachment in 1998. After leaving office he established the William J. Clinton Presidential Foundation with headquarters in Harlem, New York. A frequent lecturer, he is involved with the construction of the Clinton Library in Arkansas. He sits on the board of the International AIDS Trust as well as a variety of nonprofit organizations.

Garrett Davis

Garrett Davis, a senator from Kentucky, was born in 1801. At different points in his career Davis participated in the American (Know-Nothing), Whig, and Democratic Parties. Educated as a lawyer, he passed the bar in 1823 and ten years later was elected to the State House of Representatives.

In December 1849 he participated in efforts to revise the Kentucky constitution. Davis felt the lack of immigration restrictions was a glaring omission from the U.S. Constitution. Without restrictive laws, he feared his state would become overrun with nonwhites, which would lead to wars of race and religion.

In 1856 he declined the American Party nomination for president. A Unionist, he opposed Kentucky's secession from the United

States and served in Congress from 1861 to 1872. He died on September 22, 1872.

Marion Moncure Duncan

Marion Moncure Duncan was born on December 19, 1913. A Virginian, she graduated from the College of William and Mary in 1935. An amateur genealogist who worked as an insurance agent, Duncan participated in different civic groups and historical societies. She remained active in the Daughters of the American Revolution (DAR) throughout her life. In 1964 she was the president-general of DAR, and during the congressional debate on immigration legislation she offered her group's opinion on the importance of maintaining strict national origins quotas. She died on April 15, 1978.

Harold Fields

Nothing is known of Harold Fields other than he was enough of a recognized activist on behalf of immigrant issues that he was given air time for a national address broadcast by the National Broadcasting Company (NBC). He delivered his speech "The Alien in Our Midst" in January 1937.

Richard Gottheil

Richard James Horatio Gottheil, the son of a rabbi, was born in Manchester, England, in 1862. His family emigrated in 1873 after his father accepted a position at a temple in New York City. He graduated from Columbia College in 1881, and after five years of studies in Germany he earned his doctorate from the University of Leipzig. He became a professor of Semitic languages and eventually authored countless studies of Jewish biography, Arabic literature, and Eurasian culture. He also established the Zeta Beta Tau fraternity for Jewish students.

Gottheil and his wife, Emma, campaigned vigorously for the American Federation of Zionists, and their friendship with judges and diplomats helped their cause. He died at his New York City home in 1936.

Antonia Hernández

Antonia Hernández was born in Mexico and moved with her family to Los Angeles when she was eight years old. After earning a degree in law from UCLA she became active in the Los Angeles Center for Law and Justice. Deeply affected by her family's convictions that all people deserve equal rights, she spent a year as staff counsel for the U.S. Senate Committee on the Judiciary and joined the Mexican American Legal Defense and Education Fund (MALDEF) in 1980. She is now the organization's president and general counsel.

MALDEF, under the leadership of Hernández, organizes advocacy programs for immigrants and fights against legislation such as English-only propositions.

Eric A. Johnston

Eric Allen Johnston was born in Washington, D.C., on December 21, 1896. His family moved to Spokane, Washington, due to the poor health of his father, who died shortly thereafter. Johnston helped support his family by taking on part-time jobs and graduated from high school in 1913. He studied law at the University of Washington, and after completing his degree in 1917 he served for five years in the U.S. Marine Corps. Upon his return from military service, Johnston worked as a door-to-door salesman before investing in an electrical company that grew exponentially. He became president of two large manufacturing companies and was known as an energetic, successful leader.

Johnston also became a well-respected orator as well as the president of the U.S. Chamber of Commerce. He met with President Franklin Delano Roosevelt during World War II and organized a consortium of labor unions and business representatives to promote unity and prevent labor strikes. He died in Washington, D.C., on August 22, 1963.

John F. Kennedy

John F. Kennedy, the thirty-fifth president of the United States, was born in Brookline, Massachusetts, on May 29, 1917. The son of politician Joseph P. Kennedy and Rose Fitzgerald, Kennedy traced his ancestors from both sides of the family to Ireland. From 1935 to 1936 he attended the London School of Economics, and he graduated with honors from Harvard in 1940. While serving as a naval officer and a PT-boat commander in World War II, Kennedy earned the Purple Heart for his heroism in action.

In 1945 Kennedy worked briefly as a journalist, covering international events for newspapers such as the *Chicago Herald-American*. Two years later he was elected to the U.S. House of Representatives as a congressman from Massachusetts, and he served in this capacity for six years. In 1953 he married Jacqueline Bouvier and served his first term as senator from Massachusetts. In 1956 he authored the Pulitzer Prize–winning *Profiles in Courage*.

In 1960 Kennedy became the first Roman Catholic to be elected president. His administration was characterized by staunch anticommunism and a broadening of civil rights policies. His presidency was cut short when he was assassinated on November 22, 1963, in Dallas, Texas.

Henry Cabot Lodge

Henry Cabot Lodge was born on May 12, 1850, in Boston, Massachusetts, into a family of well-to-do New Englanders. He attended Harvard, earned his doctorate in political science, and continued his studies at Harvard Law School. He eventually became a member of the Harvard faculty and began publishing in 1876. In his writings, he extols the virtues of the early Anglo-Americans. He was known as a debater to be reckoned with who delivered and published scores of speeches.

A tireless champion of Protestant Republicanism, Lodge wrote biographies of George Washington, Alexander Hamilton, and his own great-grandfather, George Cabot. Merciless against his critics, he fought bitterly with the administration of Woodrow Wilson and played a key role in the destruction of Wilson's hope for the League of Nations.

Cabot entered politics in 1887 and spent the next thirty-seven years as a representative and senator from Massachusetts, serving as majority leader from 1918 to 1924. He died on November 9, 1924.

Edwin R. Meade

Edwin Ruthven Meade was born in New York on July 3, 1836, and died in 1889. After studying and practicing law, he was elected as a Democratic representative from New York in 1874. His most famous speeches concern the 1882 Chinese Exclusion Act, which prohibited the immigration of Chinese laborers. Meade considered these "Coolies" as monsters and saw Chinese immigration as evil.

Patsy T. Mink

Patsy Takemoto Mink was born on December 6, 1927, in Hawaii to Japanese parents. She served in the House of Representatives and made history as the first Asian American and the first woman of color elected to Congress. After the Japanese bombed Pearl Harbor in 1941, Mink and other Japanese Americans suffered a backlash of racial prejudice during World War II. She graduated valedictorian of her high school in 1944 and entered the University of Hawaii. Two years later she transferred to Nebraska, where she experienced both sexism and racism. Physically ill and unhappy with the forced segregation of the Nebraska campus, she returned to Hawaii to finish her degree.

She was admitted to the University of Chicago Law School, where she graduated in 1948. In 1951 she married John Mink, whom she had met at school. The Minks returned to Hawaii after the birth of their daughter Gwendolyn. When Patsy Mink passed the Hawaiian bar exam, she became the island's first female Japanese American lawyer. She opened a practice and taught business law at the University of Hawaii before participating in the Hawaii territorial senate and eventually running for a seat in Congress. Her successful run in 1964 led to five reelections. She died in Honolulu on September 28, 2002.

Joseph Priestley

Chemist, multilinguist, and clergyman Joseph Priestley was born in Fieldhead, England, on March 13, 1733. After the death of his mother he was raised by his aunt and was homeschooled by a Nonconformist minister. In 1755 he became a minister and traveled around the country; he tutored students in addition to preaching and experimented with natural philosophy. Six years later, while teaching languages at an academy, he took an interest in chemistry. In London in 1766 he met Benjamin Franklin, and the two worked closely together on a study of electricity. Eight years later, after much experimentation, he identified oxygen as the ingredient that passes in the metabolic cycle between animals and plants.

Priestley opposed the slave trade, publicly supported the French and American Revolutions, and dissented from the teachings of the traditional Protestant Church. In 1791, as a result of his controversial beliefs, he drew the wrath of an angry mob that burned down his house. Three years later he and his family fled England and settled in Philadelphia, Pennsylvania. He kept company with George Washington and John Adams, and he established the first Unitarian Church in America. He died in Pennsylvania on February 6, 1804.

Franklin D. Roosevelt

President Franklin Delano Roosevelt, known as FDR, was born in Hyde Park, New York, on January 30, 1882. After years of study at Harvard and Columbia, Roosevelt served in the New York Senate (1910) and then as President Woodrow Wilson's assistant secretary of the navy (1913–1924). In 1921 he contracted polio, which paralyzed his legs and confined him to a wheelchair. Seven years later he became governor of New York.

In 1933 Roosevelt became the thirty-second president of the United States, and he holds the distinction of being the only man

ever elected president four times. Within months of his inaugura-
tion he initiated the social welfare programs known as the New
Deal. During his presidency he guided the country through the
Great Depression and World War II with great compassion and humanity. He died in Georgia on April 12, 1945.

Carl Schurz

Journalist, soldier, and orator Carl Schurz was born in Liblar, Germany, on March 2, 1829. As a child he attended school in Germany, and as a young adult he participated in revolutionary upris-
ings before fleeing to Scotland. After two years in France and
England, Schurz immigrated to the United States. He first arrived
in Philadelphia and eventually relocated to Wisconsin. He participated in the antislavery movement and campaigned vigorously for
the Republican cause. He became an American citizen in the mid-
1850s. In 1856 his wife, Margaretta, founded the first kindergarten
in America.

In 1865 Schurz drafted a report exposing the reluctance of
Southerners to improve conditions for the black population. The
widespread distribution of his report influenced governmental policy on African American suffrage.

Schurz served as President Abraham Lincoln's minister to Spain
before resigning his post to become a major general in the Union
army. After the Civil War he wrote for both English and German
newspapers. In 1860 he became the first German immigrant elected
to the U.S. Senate. He died on May 14, 1906, in New York City.

Ellison DuRant Smith

Ellison DuRant Smith was born in South Carolina on August 1,
1864, on an ancestral plantation. His father's family had settled the
area, known as Tanglewood, after emigrating from England in
1747. His mother was from Scotland. Smith graduated from college in 1889 and entered politics the next year. He married in 1892
only to become a widower a year later.

In 1908 he ran an ostentatious campaign for the Senate that fea-
tured decorated mules and cotton bales. The unorthodox campaign
helped "Cotton Ed" win. Throughout his lengthy career he opposed
woman's suffrage and restrictions to child labor laws, and supported
funding of federal highways. He died on November 17, 1944.

Woodrow Wilson

Woodrow Wilson was born in Virginia in 1856. His father, a Pres-
byterian minister who had pastored in Georgia during the Civil

War, instilled in him a deep sense of morality and commitment to others. Wilson graduated from Princeton Law School before continuing his studies at the University of Virginia. After earning his doctorate at Johns Hopkins, he married Ellen Louise Axson in 1885. He taught history and political economy for seventeen years before becoming president of Princeton in 1902.

During his presidency of Princeton, Wilson earned a reputation as an educational reformer. Eight years later he was elected governor of New Jersey as a Democrat. Wilson was elected president in 1912. In 1913 Congress created the Bureau of Immigration and Naturalization. Considering the mounting international war tensions, Wilson believed it crucial that new citizens assimilate.

Wilson entered U.S. forces into World War I in 1917. At the end of the war, he unsuccessfully lobbied for the covenant of the League of Nations. In 1919, Wilson was debilitated by a stroke. He received the Nobel Peace Prize the same year. He died in 1924.

Chronology

1565
Spaniards establish Saint Augustine, Florida, as the first known settlement in North America.

1587
English colonists land on Roanoke Island, Virginia, and establish Roanoke Colony.

1598
Spain sends settlers to New Mexico and parts of Texas.

1607
Jamestown, Virginia, becomes the first permanent English settlement.

1619
The first African Americans are forcibly transported to Jamestown to work as slaves.

1620
English settlers known as Pilgrims establish Plymouth Colony after landing at Plymouth Rock, Massachusetts.

1624
Dutch settlers create the New Netherlands Colony in New York.

1638
Swedes found New Sweden, located in Delaware.

1654
The first Jews arrive in New Amsterdam (New York) as refugees from a Dutch colony in Brazil.

1683
German settlers establish Germantown near Philadelphia.

1685
Exiled French Protestants fleeing persecution immigrate to America.

1755
After forcible eviction by the British, Acadians (French-speaking Nova Scotians) move to Louisiana.

1788
The Constitution gives Congress authorization to create procedures for naturalizing citizenship for immigrants.

1790
Congress limits citizenship to "free, white" peoples.

1798
Four Alien and Sedition Acts are passed to quell opposition to President John Adams; the Alien Act expires in 1800, and others are repealed or not renewed.

1845
The potato famine in Ireland forces more than 1.6 million Irish to America.

1848–1849
The first Chinese immigration to the United States; many settle in California.

1854
The Know-Nothing Party, an anti-immigrant movement, reaches its peak of influence and power.

1868
The Fourteenth Amendment grants citizenship rights to "all persons born or naturalized in the United States."

1870
Japanese laborers immigrate, many settling in California. The Naturalization Act of 1870 establishes citizenship rights for "persons of African Descent."

1882
Passage of the Chinese Exclusion Act halts Chinese immigration. The act also imposes an immigrant head tax and sets the groundwork for the creation of the Immigration and Naturalization Service (INS).

1886
The Statue of Liberty is dedicated.

1892
Ellis Island opens as a way station for arriving immigrants.

1905–1914
More than 10 million immigrants arrive in America.

1907
The so-called Gentlemen's Agreement signed by the United States and Japan restricts Japanese immigration.

1910
According to the U.S. Census, the total U.S. population is 92 million, with 13.5 million people identified as immigrants.

1917
The Immigration Act of 1917 expands the list of banned foreigners, imposes a literacy test, and prohibits the immigration of mentally deficient people and political subversives.

1921
The Emergency Quota Act is passed; quotas of national origin are determined with broadly restrictive effects.

1924
A swell of popular nativism culminates with the Johnson-Reed Act, also known as the Immigration Act of 1924. Restrictions of the 1921 act are stiffened, and the emergency quotas are made permanent.

1939–1945
Immigration is curtailed by the events of World War II.

Refugee Jews in Europe, including children, are denied entry into the United States.

1942

To supplement the labor shortage created by World War II deployments, the United States creates a program to import workers from Mexico called the bracero program.

The internment of Japanese Americans begins.

1943

The Chinese Exclusion Act is repealed.

1952

The McCarran-Walter Act of 1952 (also known as the Immigration and Nationality Act) reaffirms national origins quotas. Other provisions include new political tests for immigrants and expansion of the authority of the Border Patrol.

1954

Ellis Island closes.

"Operation Wetback" deports more than 2 million Mexicans and Mexican Americans.

1960

Cubans flee after dictator Fidel Castro takes power, and a Cuban refugee policy is established.

1963

Vietnamese, Cambodians, and Laotians begin arriving from Southeast Asia; war refugees arrive in great numbers for the next twenty years.

1964

The bracero program officially ends.

1965

President Lyndon Johnson effectively ends the quota system when he signs the Immigration and Nationality Act amendments into law.

1980
The Refugee Act of 1980 establishes the first official system for admitting refugees, amends the official definition of a refugee, and outlines procedures to assist displaced persons with domestic resettlement.

1986
Congress passes the Immigration Reform and Control Act, which criminalizes the hiring of illegal immigrants and provides a onetime amnesty for immigrants who had lived in the United States continuously since 1982.

1990
The Immigration Act of 1990 grants visa preferences to workers whose skills are in high demand.

2001
The events of September 11 dramatically alter U.S. immigration policy. The INS is widely criticized for mishandling the visa applications of the hijackers.

2003
Citing national security reasons, government officials detain Arabs and Arab American citizens at the Guantánamo Bay military detention center. The Department of Homeland Security is established in January. Under the direction of this new department, the Bureau of Citizenship and Immigration Services is established after the name "INS" is officially abolished.

For Further Research

EDITH ABBOTT, ED., *Historical Aspects of the Immigration Problem*. New York: Arno Press, 1969.

JUDITH BENTLEY, *American Immigration Today: Pressures, Problems, Policies*. New York: J. Messner, 1981.

HENRY BISCHOFF, *Immigration Issues*. Westport, CT: Greenwood Press, 2002.

PETER BRIMELOW, *Alien Nation: Common Sense About America's Immigration Disaster*. New York: Random House, 1995.

WESLEY BROWN AND AMY LING, EDS., *Visions of America: Personal Narratives from the Promised Land*. New York: Persea Books, 1993.

NICHOLAS CAPALDI, ED., *Immigration: Debating the Issues*. New York: Prometheus Books, 1997.

SUCHENG CHAN, *Entry Denied: Exclusion and the Chinese Community in America, 1882–1943*. Philadelphia: Temple University Press, 1991.

KO-LIN CHIN, *Smuggled Chinese: Clandestine Immigration to the United States*. Philadelphia: Temple University Press, 1999.

JAMES CIMENT, ED., *Encyclopedia of American Immigration*. 4 vols. Armonk, NY: M.E. Sharpe, 2001.

ROGER DANIELS, *American Immigration: A Student Companion*. New York: Oxford University Press, 2001.

MERI NANA-AMA DANQUAH, ED., *Becoming American: Personal Essays by First Generation Immigrant Women*. New York: Hyperion, 2000.

LEONARD DINNERSTEIN AND DAVID M. REIMERS, *Ethnic Americans: A History of Immigration*. New York: Columbia University Press, 1999.

WILLIAM DUDLEY, ED., *Illegal Immigration: Opposing Viewpoints.* San Diego, CA: Greenhaven Press, 2002.

ALICE MOORE DUNBAR, ED., *Masterpieces of Negro Eloquence.* New York: G.K. Hall, 1997.

RONALD FERNANDEZ, *America's Banquet of Cultures: Harnessing Ethnicity, Race, and Immigration in the Twenty-First Century.* Westport, CT: Praeger, 2000.

JON GJERDE, ED., *Major Problems in American Immigration and Ethnic History.* New York: Houghton Mifflin, 1998.

NATHAN GLAZER, ED., *Clamor at the Gates: The New American Immigration.* San Francisco: ICS Press, 1985.

CAMILLE GUERIN-GONZALES, *Mexican Workers and American Dreams: Immigration, Repatriation, and California Farm Labor, 1900–1939.* New Brunswick, NJ: Rutgers University Press, 1994.

DAVID W. HAINES AND CAROL A. MORTLAND, EDS., *Manifest Destinies: Americanizing Immigrants and Internationalizing Americans.* Westport, CT: Praeger, 2001.

JOHN F. KENNEDY, *A Nation of Immigrants.* New York: Harper and Row, 1964.

RICHARD D. LAMM AND GARY IMHOFF, *The Immigration Time Bomb: The Fragmenting of America.* New York: Truman Talley Books, 1985.

ANN CHIH LIN, ED., *Immigration.* Washington, DC: CQ Press, 2002.

CALVIN MCLEOD LOGUER, ED., *Representative American Speeches, 1937–1997.* New York: H.W. Wilson, 1997.

BRIAN MACARTHUR, ED., *The Penguin Book of Twentieth-Century Speeches.* New York: Penguin Books, 1994.

JOEL MILLMAN, *The Other Americans: How Immigrants Renew Our Country, Our Economy, and Our Values.* New York: Viking Press, 1997.

ALEJANDRO PORTES, ED., *The New Second Generation*. New York: Russell Sage Foundation, 1996.

JORGE RAMOS, *The Other Face of America: Chronicles of the Immigrants Shaping Our Future*. Trans. Patricia J. Duncan. New York: HarperCollins, 2002.

ROBERT A. ROCKAWAY, ED., *Words of the Uprooted: Jewish Immigrants in Early Twentieth-Century America*. Ithaca, NY: Cornell University Press, 1998.

TAMARA L. ROLEFF, ED., *Immigration: Opposing Viewpoints*. San Diego, CA: Greenhaven Press, 1998.

PETER I. ROSE, *Tempest-Tost: Race, Immigration, and the Dilemmas of Diversity*. New York: Oxford University Press, 1997.

DENNIS ELLIOTT SHASHA AND MARINA SHRON, *Red Blues: Voices from the Last Wave of Russian Immigrants*. New York: Holmes & Meier, 2002.

JAMES P. SMITH AND BARRY EDMONSTON, EDS., *The Immigration Debate*. Washington, DC: National Academy Press, 1998.

DEBORAH G. STRAUB, ED., *Voices of Multicultural America: Notable Speeches Delivered by African, Asian, Hispanic, and Native Americans, 1790–1995*. Detroit: Gale Research, 1996.

REED UEDA, *Postwar Immigrant America: A Social History*. Boston: St. Martin's Press, 1994.

DENNIS WEPMAN, *Immigration: From the Founding of Virginia to the Closing of Ellis Island*. New York: Facts On File, 2002.

NORMAN L. ZUCKER AND NAOMI FLINK ZUCKER, *Desperate Crossings: Seeking Refuge in America*. Armonk, NY: M.E. Sharpe, 1996.

Websites

American Memory Project, http://lcweb2.loc.gov/ammem/ ammemhome.html. This Library of Congress website includes an extensive collection of immigration documents, photos, and historical records.

Bureau of Citizenship and Immigration Services, www.bcis. gov. The official website of the former Department of Immigration and Naturalization Services (INS).

Center for Immigration Studies, www.cis.org. Tax exempt think tank that publishes reports supporting reduced immigration.

Immigration and Refugee Services of America, www. irsa-uscr.org. This organization assists immigrants and refugees through the development of educational programs. Links to news articles and photo galleries are available.

National Immigration Forum, www.immigrationforum.org. Non-profit organization that advocates for immigration and immigrants' rights.

Index